1983

Teaching Elementary
School Science
Through Motor Learning

Teaching Elementary School Science Through Motor Learning

By

JAMES H. HUMPHREY

Professor of Physical Education and
Motor Activity Learning Specialist
University of Maryland
College Park, Maryland

With a Foreword by

Henry H. Walbesser

Professor and Assistant Dean
Graduate Studies and Research
College of Education
University of Maryland
College Park, Maryland

CHARLES C THOMAS • PUBLISHER
Springfield • Illinois • U.S.A.

Published and Distributed Throughout the World by

CHARLES C THOMAS • PUBLISHER

Bannerstone House

301-327 East Lawrence Avenue, Springfield, Illinois, U.S.A.

© *1975, by* CHARLES C THOMAS • PUBLISHER

ISBN 0-398-03252-1

Library of Congress Catalog Card Number: 00 00000

With THOMAS BOOKS careful attention is given to all details of
manufacturing and design. It is the Publisher's desire to present books that are
satisfactory as to their physical qualities and artistic possibilities and
appropriate for their particular use. THOMAS BOOKS will be true to those
laws of quality that assure a good name and good will.

Printed in the United States of America
R-1

Library of Congress Cataloging in Publication Data

Humphrey, James Harry, 1911-
    Teaching elementary school science through motor
learning.

    1. Science—Study and teaching (Elementary)
2. Motor learning. I. Title. [DNLM: 1. Learning.
2. In infancy & childhood—Science. 3. Education—
Teaching. LB1585 H926t]
LB1585.H78   372.3'5'044   74-9732
ISBN 0-398-03252-1

FOREWORD

IT is a great privilege to have been asked to write a foreword to the fine book you are about to read and use. A privilege because this *is* a book of exceptional worth. Hence, there is both personal and professional satisfaction in being able to praise its virtues.

Integration of formerly disassociated fields of study is a dominant characteristic of the sign of our times. Professor Humphrey has achieved the exciting integration of movement in physical space with the study of elementary science, a unifying of physical education and science.

In this book, the author has constructed a theoretical foundation which can guide the teacher and has described a process for applying the theory with specific instructional strategies. Each concept is clearly developed with excellent examples. However, this is not a "Cookbook" to be followed without question. The assumption is clear throughout the book that the process is a creative one in which each teacher formulates the actions he or she deems appropriate for each instructional setting. The book guides; it does not command.

This description of theory and practice which blends the advantages of two fields for the benefit of more effective instruction will be helpful and provocative to any teacher. Most especially, this will be a welcomed volume for those teachers who view their function to be one of assisting students to develop skill in seeking an understanding of the world about them.

HENRY H. WALBESSER

v

PREFACE

CHILD learning through motor activity has received a great deal of recognition in recent years, and increasing attention of educators is being directed to this social psychological phenomenon. The use of motor activity as a medium of learning is not only supported by respectable theoretical postulation but is backed up by sophisticated research as well. *Teaching Elementary School Science Through Motor Learning* has been developed with this basic premise in mind.

The introductory chapter gives an overview of the development of the science program in elementary schools over the years. Chapter Two explains the theory of motor activity learning, while Chapter Three suggests some general ways in which science learning experiences can be provided through motor activity. Chapter Four takes into account some objective evidence for the approach as it applies to elementary school science. A technique for combining reading with science is dealt with in Chapter Five. Chapter Six considers how motor activity learning might be employed with slow learning children. The final three chapters contain over fifty motor activities in which science concepts are inherent in such broad areas of study as the universe and earth, conditions of life, and chemical and physical changes.

The book should have a variety of uses. It could serve as a supplementary text in teacher preparation courses in Teaching Elementary School Science. It could be helpful in certain teacher preparation courses in Special Education. Finally, it should be valuable as a handbook of science learning activities for classroom teachers.

The materials contained in the text have undergone extensive field trials in various types of situations. The author is most grateful to the many teachers who tried out the materials and made valuable suggestions for their use. Special acknowledgment is due to Dr. Harvey Hall, Supervisor of Science, Prince Georges County. Maryland Public Schools, for his advice on certain aspects of the book.

College Park, Maryland   J. H. H.

CONTENTS

Teaching Elementary
School Science
Through Motor Learning

INTRODUCTION

....

THE EVOLVING NATURE OF
ELEMENTARY SCHOOL SCIENCE

During the past several decades the science program in the elementary school has been characterized by widely divergent practices. This can perhaps be accounted for in part by the changing needs of society as well as the needs of individuals within the society. In this particular regard, one needs to consider the question as to how much the demands of society should be taken into account as related to the needs of the individual. Various points of view have been expressed in this particular connection. One school of thought tends to hold that, because the schools are publicly supported to serve the needs of society, the curriculum content should be based primarily on factors oriented in a direction to meet these societal needs. A second point of view suggests that, inasmuch as it is the purpose of schools to educate the individual, the curriculum should be based upon the needs of individuals. A rather obvious third point of view involves some sort of happy medium between the first two. This is based on the fact that the individual is a part of society and that he should be educated with the idea in mind that he will interact with it. It is apparent that those who have had the responsibility of providing desirable and worthwhile learning experiences in science for elementary school children have had to cope with this problem. And, this will perhaps be readily discerned in the following discussions in this introductory chapter.

PAST PRACTICES IN ELEMENTARY SCHOOL SCIENCE

In the early decades of the nineteenth century, what passed for science in the early common schools consisted of certain *wonders of the supernatural.* This is to say that teachers were expected to convey information to children that might help them to appreciate the various aspects of nature. Children were not expected to understand that there were natural causes for certain things that happened, but rather to believe that some mysterious application of a higher power was enough of an explanation for things that occurred.

About mid-nineteenth century some aspects of educational philosophy abroad began to make an impact on American education. An example of this was the Pestalozzian schools which expounded the theories of the great Swiss educator Heinrich Pestalozzi (1746-1827). He has been credited by many with laying the foundation for the modern concept of basing curriculum content upon knowledge of growth and development of children.

Educators of the time tended to interpret Pestalozzi's philosophy as one that involved an instructional procedure that became known as *object teaching.* The purpose of this approach, as far as science was concerned, was for children to observe certain objects under the detailed directions given by the teacher. Children were expected to memorize various details about these objects. Properties of the objects were observed in a sequence with little or no regard as to how one particular object might be related to another. Perhaps the reason for this was that in those days the belief was still held that children were not able to understand such relationships. Of all of the weaknesses of such an approach, it had at least one aspect to commend it. This was that in object teaching, the actual objects studied needed to be available for the children to see and manipulate.

Object teaching prevailed as the predominant method of providing information about science to elementary school children until about 1870, the approximate onset of the industrial revolution in the United States. It has been suggested that at about this time in American history, science education through object teaching was waning because this approach was not meeting the needs of children. It was replaced by nature study; this aspect of science in elementary education continued for about a half century. A part of the basis for this has been attributed to the notion that there was "a desire to improve the lagging agricultural economy and to prevent the accumulation of unemployed rural migrants in the city." (1)

In actual practice the nature study approach did not differ appreciably from object teaching. It appeared that the basic idea of nature study was to help children develop an understanding and life-long appreciation of nature. The extent to which this was accomplished by the approach used has been open to question, but nevertheless the practice continued until shortly after World War I.

In the middle Twenties a newer concept of science education was introduced into many elementary schools of America. This approach was referred to as the doctrine of social utility. This meant generally that science should be considered in terms of its practical application in solving certain problems that had to be encountered in daily living. It is interesting to note that in a number of instances this approach is in effect at the present time, although it is being subjected to continuing criticism as witnessed by the following representative statement:

> Recent events indicate that our continuing attempts to deal with the expanding body of scientific knowledge will become less and less effective unless two new emphases replace the traditional goal of mastery of the facts and details of a subject field. First, subject fields need to be reduced more efficiently to their fundamental structure, enabling students to master those few conceptual schemes around which many kinds of facts and details can be logically organized as they are needed. Second, students need to learn the processes by which knowledge is acquired in science; that is they need to "learn how to learn" in order to cope with the accelerating rate of change. The doctrine of social utility has provided neither the skills in the processes of science nor the conceptual framework necessary for understanding future developments in an expanding field of study. (2)

The transition of methods and content in any subject area is not likely to be characterized by sharp lines of demarcation. Such is the case with elementary school science because the transition from the doctrine of social utility has been occurring over a period of years and in fact, is still in the process. One of the highlights in

1. Wm. Vernon Hicks and others, *The New Elementary School Curriculum* (New York, Van Nostrand Reinhold Company, 1970), p. 91.
2. *Ibid.*, p. 92.

this transition period occurred in the late 1940's when action was taken by the National Council for the Study of Education. The Forty-Sixth Yearbook of the Council stated that:

> children should by the end of each year . . . have experienced growth in the broader areas of *physical* and *biological* environment, such as the following:
>
> *The Universe:* Study of the stars, the sun, the moon, the planets and their inter-relationships; causes of day and night, seasonal changes, tides, eclipses, and (less-completely) of the vastness of the Milky Way and of galactic systems beyond our own.
>
> *The Earth:* Origin, formation of mountains, weathering of rock into soil, erosion, volcanism, prehistoric life, and the forces that are changing and have changed the earth.
>
> *Conditions Necessary to Life:* What living things need in order to exist, how they are affected by changes in the environment and the struggle for existence.
>
> *Living Things:* Variety, social life, adaptations for protection, life cycles of plants and animals, how they obtain food, their economic importance, and man's influence upon nature.
>
> *Physical and Chemical Phenomena:* Common chemical and physical phenomena such as light, sound, gravity, magnetism, and electricity; changes in matter; and the phenomena associated with radiant energy and atmospheric changes.
>
> *Man's Attempt to Control His Environment:* In gardens, on farms, in orchards, inventions and discoveries; use of power and of minerals; his control over living things; his study of places he cannot reach directly; and other such topics. (3)

In the early 1950's, experts in the area of elementary school science were advocating a shift away from the type of curriculum offering that was based merely on satisfying curiosity, and suggesting that the trend should be in the direction of providing learning experiences in science that were of real concern in the lives of children. This was described by Blough and Blackwood as follows:

> Science in the grade school. What is it? First of all it's *not* a lot of things it was once thought to be. It's not a series of object lessons about a piece of granite, an old wasp's nest, an acorn, or a tulip. It's

3. National Society for the Study of Education: *Forty-Sixth Yearbook,* Part I, Science Education in American Schools (Chicago, University of Chicago Press, 1947), pp. 75-76.

not hit and miss like that. It's not learning the names of the parts of a grasshopper or of a trillium. It's not learning to identify 20 trees, 20 insects, 20 flowers, or 20 anything else.

What is it, then? It's a study of the problems that are found wherever children live. More formally stated, it is a study of the natural environment. It's not pieces of chemistry and physics and biology and astronomy and geology. Its content comes from these areas, but it's a study of problems that pop into curious children's minds as they live and grow from one day to the next, like: What makes the wind blow? What's in a cloud? What's a stone made of? What does a bell do when it rings? How can a seed grow into a tree? What makes a rainbow? Anyone who has ever visited with grade-school girls and boys knows that most of them are chockful of questions like this and generally they like to know the answers to them. Well, finding the answers — that's science. (4)

During that same general time frame many educators still tended to feel that the teaching of science was being grossly underemphasized in the elementary school. For instance, Herrick indicated that "most science programs are limited to the reading of some science text with children; most science periods are seldom more than twenty minutes; few classrooms have any science equipment." (5)

This belief was further supported by Beck, Cook, and Kearney when they stated:

In many instances, the absence of aquariums, herbariums, low-power microscopes, magnifying glasses, magnets, batteries, test tubes, and other elementary scientific equipment in the classroom is in itself indicative of the fact that the teaching of science is neglected. Usually, the elementary teacher needs more help in the teaching of science than he needs in teaching music, art, and physical education. In the elementary school, the teaching of science is not likely to improve greatly until school administrators and the public begin to recognize its value and importance. (6)

------

4. Glenn O. Blough and Paul E. Blackwood, *Teaching Elementary Science* (Washington, D.C., Department of Health, Education and Welfare, Office of Education, 1954), p. 2.
5. Virgil E. Herrick, *Issues in Elementary Education* (Minneapolis, Burgess Publishing Company, 1952), p. 153.
6. Robert H. Beck, Walter W. Cook, and Nolan C. Kearney, *Curriculum in the Modern Elementary School* (New York, Prentice-Hall, 1953), pp. 284-285.

Perhaps the greatest single incident which provided the most impact for science education at all educational levels in America was the occasion of the Soviet Union's launching of the sputnik in October 1957. As a result of this, unprecedented interest was generated in science in the elementary school, and responsible groups and individuals were spurred to action to improve curriculum offerings.

RECENT DEVELOPMENTS IN THE
ELEMENTARY SCHOOL SCIENCE CURRICULUM

As a result of the impetus that elementary school science has been receiving, a new era of curriculum development began to get under way in the early 1960's. The felt need for better programs of science in elementary schools stimulated action to embark upon a number of curriculum projects. In this endeavor it became a rather common practice for scientists and educators to join forces in developing these projects, many of which were funded by the National Science Foundation. Among various others, these projects include the following:

1. COPES, Conceptually Oriented Program in Elementary Science, New York University, New York, New York.

2. Elementary School Science by a Quantitative Approach, State University of New York, Stony Brook, New York.

3. Elementary School Science Project, University of California, Berkeley, California.

4. Elementary School Science Project, Utah State University, Logan, Utah.

5. Elementary Science Study, Educational Development Center, Inc., 55 Chapel Street, Newton, Massachusetts. (Materials published by: McGraw-Hill Book Company, Webster Division, Manchester, Missouri)

6. MINNEMAST, Minnesota School Mathematics and Science Center, 720 Washington Avenue, S. E., Minneapolis, Minnesota.

7. Science — A Process Approach, Commission on Science Education, American Association for the Advancement of Science, 1515 Massachusetts Avenue, N. W., Washington, D. C. (Materials published by: Xerox Education Division, 600 Madison Avenue,

New York, New York)

8. Science Curriculum Improvement Study, Department of Physics, University of California, Berkeley, California. (Materials published by: Rand McNally, P.O. Box 7600, Chicago, Illinois)

9. WIMSA, Webster Institute of Mathematics, Science and the Arts, Webster College, 470 East Lockwood Street, St. Louis, Missouri.

While all of the projects differ in many ways, it might be said of them that they are possibly more alike than they are different. This is to say that there are certain basic characteristics that are inherent in all of them. Two of these constant features which have the utmost pertinence to the present text are 1) that children should become involved insofar as possible in concrete kinds of learning experiences, and 2) that the learning experiences be child centered. As will be seen in subsequent chapters, learning through motor activity is made to order for this kind of procedure. For example, motor activity learning experiences in the area of science are so concrete that they become a part of the child's physical reality. And as for these kinds of activities being child centered, children actually engage in movement experiences where science concepts are inherent.

CURRENT PRACTICES IN ELEMENTARY SCHOOL SCIENCE

Despite the fact that a major effort has been made to initiate changes in the elementary school science curriculum, implementation as far as the various curriculum revision projects is concerned has not been extensive. Possibly the primary reason for this is the apprehension that there may develop a trend toward a national curriculum in science.

As in the case of many other curriculum areas in the elementary school, local school systems tend to provide for their own specific science curriculum. These of course range from poor to outstanding programs, depending upon the available natural corollaries needed for success in such programs.

A constant characteristic of most local programs is that they tend to arrive at some sort of scope and sequence which best meet the needs at the local level. Scope is concerned with the science learning experiences to be provided (concepts to be developed), and sequence refers to the grade placement of such experiences. There is a relatively high degree of agreement as to the major areas of study for science, but agreement is not necessarily found as far as sequence is concerned.

It is also interesting to note that there are a variety of ways which are used to organize and provide for science learning experiences in the elementary school. In general, these include 1) science as a separate subject, 2) separate science units, 3) utilizing science opportunities when they occur, and 4) incorporating science experiences in large units of study, as in the social studies.

It is not the purpose here to either extol or criticize any of the existing plans of organization in the elementary school science program. On the contrary, the point of view is taken that learning through motor activity is most compatible with the way in which children learn, as well as with other aspects of their growth and development. With this general frame of reference in mind, the thrust of the text will be in the direction of how this medium of learning can be utilized in the development and understanding of science concepts.

THE NATURE OF LEARNING
THROUGH MOTOR ACTIVITY

MEANING OF MOTOR LEARNING

THE term *motor learning* has been defined in a number of ways. Most of these definitions are more alike than they are different, tending to center around the general idea that motor learning is concerned only with the learning of motor skills. As an example, the *Dictionary of Education* differentiates between what might be termed *ideational* learning and *motor* learning in the following manner: "Ideational learning is concerned with ideas, concepts, and mental associations, while motor learning is that in which the learner achieves new facility in the performance of bodily movements as a result of specific practice." (7) Although this may be a convenient and simple description of motor learning, it does not serve the purpose adequately in modern times. The reason for this is that motor learning can no longer be considered a unilateral entity. At one time, when thought of only in terms of learning motor skills, it might have been considered by some as almost the exclusive purview of the physical educator and psychologist. However, it has now become such a multiphasic area that it compels the interest and attention of a variety of professions and disciplines.

Various aspects of motor learning in one way or another are involved in such fields as physical education, psychology, psychiatry, and neurophysiology. In fact, in almost any endeavor of human concern that one might mention, some aspect of motor learning could play a very significant part. It is for this reason that we no longer think of motor learning only in the sense of the previously mentioned definition. Consequently, some attempt

7. Carter V. Good, *Dictionary of Education,* 2d ed. (New York, McGraw-Hill, 1959), p. 314.

needs to be made to identify certain branches of specific aspects of motor learning. This is the case with the present volume, *Teaching Elementary School Science Through Motor Learning.*

Branches of Motor Learning

In order to put this particular topic in its proper perspective and to establish a suitable frame of reference for subsequent discussions of it, we will identify three aspects of motor learning. (8) It should be understood that these identifications are used arbitrarily for our own purpose. Others may identify these differently, and in the absence of anything resembling standardized terminology, it is their prerogative to do so. Moreover, it is also recognized that some individuals might wish to segment these aspects of motor learning further, or add others. With this is mind we will identify the three aforementioned aspects as follows:

1. Motor learning which is concerned essentially with conditions surrounding the *learning of motor skills.*

2. Motor learning which is concerned essentially with *perceptual motor development.* (This may also be referred to as *psychomotor development* or *neuromotor perceptual training.*)

3. Motor learning which is concerned essentially with *academic skill and concept development.*

It should be clearly understood that all of the above areas of motor learning involve the same general concept, and that there are various degrees of interrelatedness and interdependence of each area upon the other.

Motor Learning Involving the Learning of Motor Skills

This branch of motor learning has commanded the attention of individuals in the field of physical education mainly because it forms the basic citadel for subject matter and methods of teaching in this field. Some of the areas in which attention has been

---

8. To our knowledge this particular classification of motor learning was first introduced into the literature as follows: James H. Humphrey, "Academic Skill and Concept Development Through Motor Activity," *The Academy Papers,* No. 1, The American Academy of Physical Education (1968), pp. 29-35.

centered include: how individuals learn motor skills, length and distribution of practice, mechanical principles, transfer, and retention. Research in some of these areas by some physical educators has been outstanding and, as might be expected, it has been done primarily by those who have some background in psychology.

In recent years it appears that there has been more compatibility between psychologists and physical educators regarding this branch of motor learning. The fact that such has not always been the case is suggested in the following comment by one psychologist.

> There is one perhaps distressing feature which is apparent: this is the seeming lack of awareness which the two disciplines have of the progress *and* problems of the other's area. (9)

Fortunately there is evidence of amelioration of this condition because more and more, psychologists are discovering that physical education and sports experiences provide an excellent natural climate and laboratory for the study of human performance and behavior. We should mention again that this aspect was the only subject of definition of motor learning in the *Dictionary of Education.* Moreover, it will *not* be the function of the present text to deal with this branch of motor learning as such. There are a number of fine books devoted entirely to this branch of motor learning which may be found in most major libraries.

Motor Learning Involving Perceptual Motor Development

This branch of motor learning involves the correction, or at least some degree of improvement, of certain motor deficiencies, especially those associated with fine coordinations. An example of the need for this type of training may be seen with certain neurologically handicapped children who may have various types of learning disorders. What some specialists have identified as a perceptual-motor deficit syndrome is said to exist in such cases. An attempt may be made to correct or improve fine motor control problems through a carefully developed sequence of motor

9. G. B. Johnson, "Motor Learning," in. W. R. Johnson, ed., *Science and Medicine of Exercise and Sports* (New York, Harper and Brothers, 1960), p. 602.

competencies, which follow a definite hierarchy of development. This may occur through either structured or unstructured programs. As far as physical education is concerned, this branch of motor learning might be thought of as education *of* the physical.

In recent years various aspects of this area of motor learning have contributed to the alleviation of certain types of learning disorders in children. It should be apparent that a wide range of specialists and disciplines are needed to help children effectively through this area of motor learning. We previously called attention to certain areas of speciality which in one way or another can make important contributions. Again it will *not* be the function of this volume to explore this dimension of motor learning. However, there is a rather substantial body of literature listed in the various educational indices which the interested reader may pursue in the area of perceptual motor development.

Motor Learning Involving Academic Skill and Concept Development Through Motor Activity

This might also be referred to as the physical education learning medium. This branch of motor learning is concerned specifically with children learning basic skills and concepts in the various subject areas in the elementary school curriculum through the medium of motor activity. (Whereas motor learning involving perceptual motor development was thought of in terms of education *of* the physical, this aspect of motor learning is concerned with education *through* the physical.) The focus and thrust of the present volume will be on the contribution this aspect of motor learning can make to child learning of concepts in science.

It may be interesting to note that one well-known psychologist, Dr. James J. Asher, has identified this branch of motor learning as "total physical response motor learning." Asher suggests that research in motor learning is usually done with tasks which involve *parts* of the body — the receptors and effectors — as illustrated in display-control problems, rather than with the whole body. His work with the total physical response technique has been done in the area of learning foreign language and essentially involves having students listen to a command in a foreign language and immediately respond with the appropriate physical action. In connection with our work, Asher comments as follows:

> The work that comes closest to total physical response motor learning is Humphrey's investigations of learning through games in which, for example, the acquisition of certain reading skills was significantly accelerated when the learning task occurred in the context of a game involving the entire body. (10)

THE THEORY OF LEARNING THROUGH MOTOR ACTIVITY

The idea of motor activity learning is not new. In fact, the application of motor activity was a basic principle of the Froebelian kindergarten and was based on the theory that children learn and acquire information, understanding, and skills through motor activities in which they are naturally interested, such as building, constructing, modeling, painting and various forms of movement.

Movement is one of the most fundamental characteristics of life. Whatever else they may involve, all of man's achievements are based upon his ability to move. Obviously, the very young child is not an intelligent being in the sense of performing abstract thinking, and he only gradually acquires the ability to deal with symbols and intellectualize his experiences in the course of his development. On the other hand, the child is a creature of movement and feeling. Any efforts to educate the child must take this relative dominance of the intellectual versus movement and feeling into account. Furthermore, by engaging in movement experiences to develop academic skills and concepts, these skills and concepts become a part of the child's physical reality.

When we speak of motor activity learning in the present text, we refer to things that children *do* actively in a pleasurable situation in order to learn. This should suggest to teachers that motor learning activities can be derived from basic physical education curriculum content found in such broad categories as game activities, rhythmic activities, and self-testing activities.

10. James J. Asher, "The Total Physical Response Technique of Learning," *Journal of Special Education* (Fall, 1969).

Hence, our reason for indicating previously that learning through motor activity can also be referred to as the physical education learning medium. Classroom teachers and physical education teachers might well team up to facilitate learning and development of skills in their respective areas of responsibility through an integrated and cross-reinforcement program.

This brings up an important point for consideration, that is the function of the classroom teacher and physical education teacher in the use and implementation of motor activity learning. It has been mentioned before that motor activity learning experience can be derived from physical education content. However, physical education should be considered a subject "in its own right" in the elementary school curriculum with the natural corollaries of good teaching, sufficient facilities and the like. Consequently, the use of motor activity as a learning medium in other subject areas — in this case science — should not ordinarily occur during the regular time allotted to physical education. On the other hand, this approach should be considered as a way of learning science in the same way that other kinds of learning activities are used in this subject. This means that, for the most part, this procedure, when it is used, should be employed during the regularly allotted time for science. Perhaps the ideal situation would prevail when the classroom teacher and physical education teacher work closely together in the use of this approach. The classroom teacher knows the science concepts to be developed and the physical education teacher should have a thorough knowledge of the various physical education activities that might be useful in developing these concepts.

This aspect of motor learning is based essentially on the theory that children — being predominantly movement oriented — will learn better when what we will arbitrarily call *academic learning* takes place through pleasurable physical activity; that is, when the motor component operates at a maximum level in skill and concept development in school subject areas essentially oriented to so-called verbal learning. This is not to say that motor and verbal learning are two mutually exclusive kinds of learning, although it has been suggested that, at the two extremes, the dichotomy appears justifiable. It is recognized that in verbal learning which involves almost complete abstract symbolic manipulations, there may be, among others, such motor components as tension, subvocal speech, and physiological changes in metabolism which operate at a minimal level. It is also recognized that in physical education activities where the learning is predominantly motor in nature, verbal learning is evident, although perhaps at a minimal level. For example, in teaching a physical education activity there is a certain amount of verbalization in developing a kinesthetic concept of the particular activity that is being taught.

One way in which motor activity learning is used to teach science involves the selection of a physical education activity in which a science concept is inherent. The activity is taught to the children and used as a learning activity for the development of a science concept. An attempt is made to arrange an active learning situation so that a concept is being acted out, practiced or rehearsed in the course of participating in the physical education activity. In this procedure it is theorized that the concept is removed from the realm of the abstract and becomes a part of the child's physical reality. Let us consider an example. This example involves the concept: Electricity travels along a pathway and needs a complete circuit over which to travel. The activity to develop the concept is Straddle Ball Roll. The group is divided into four or more smaller groups. The children of each group stand one behind the other in single file. All are in stride position, with feet far enough apart so that a ball can be rolled between the legs of the players. The first person in each file holds a rubber playground ball. At a signal, the person in front of each file starts the activity by attempting to roll the ball between the legs of all the children in his file. The team that gets the ball to the last member of the file first in the manner described, scores a point. The last player goes to the head of the file and this procedure is continued, with a point scored each time for the team that gets the ball back to the last player first. After every player has had the opportunity to roll the ball back, the team which has scored the most points is declared the winner. An application of this would be as follows: The first player at the head of each file becomes the electric switch which opens and shuts the circuit. The ball is the electric current. As the ball rolls between the children's legs, it moves right through if all legs are in proper lineup. When a leg is not in the proper stride, the path of the ball is impeded and the ball rolls out. The game has to be stopped until the ball is recovered and the correction made in the position of the leg. The circuit (that is, the child's leg) has to be repaired before the flow of electricity (which is the path of the ball) can be resumed.

In one specific situation in which this activity was used to help develop the particular concept, the teacher reported that the children were quick to see and make the analogy themselves after seeing how the interference in the path of the ball sent it out of bounds and stopped the game. In similar fashion any blockage of an electric circuit would break the current and stop the flow of electricity. They gave this variation of the game a new name, Keep the Circuit Closed.

It is interesting to note that in this particular case an experiment with wired batteries and a bell was also used in connection with the development of this concept. Some children reported that they understood this better after they had played Straddle Ball Roll because they could actually *see* the electric current which in this case was the ball. (A large number of these kinds of learning activities will be presented in subsequent chapters.)

FACTORS INFLUENCING LEARNING
THROUGH MOTOR ACTIVITY

During the early school years, and at ages six to eight particularly, it is possible that learning is limited frequently by a relatively short attention span rather than only by intellectual capabilities. Moreover, some children who do not appear to think or learn well in abstract terms can more readily grasp concepts when given an opportunity to use them in an applied manner. In view of the fact that the child is a creature of movement and also that he is likely to deal better in concrete rather than abstract terms, it would seem to follow naturally that the motor activity medium is well suited for him.

The above statement should not be interpreted to mean that the author is suggesting that learning through movement oriented experiences (motor learning) and passive learning experiences (verbal learning) are two different kinds of learning. The position is taken here that learning is learning, even though as stated previously, in the motor activity approach the motor component may be operating at a higher level than in most of the traditional types of learning activities.

The theory of learning accepted here is that learning takes place in terms of reorganization of the systems of perception into a functional and integrated whole because of the result of certain stimuli. This implies that problem solving is the way of human learning and that learning takes place through problem solving. In a motor activity learning situation that is well planned, a great deal of consideration should be given to the inherent possibilities for learning in terms of problem solving. In this approach opportunities abound for near-ideal teaching-learning situations because of the many problems to be solved. Using active games as an example, the following representative questions asked by children indicate that there is a great opportunity for reflective thinking, use of judgment, and problem solving in this type of experience.

1. Why didn't I get to touch the ball more often?
2. How can we make it a better game?
3. Would two circles be better than one?
4. What were some of the things you liked about the game?
5. How can I learn to throw the ball better?

Another very important factor to consider with respect to this approach is that a considerable part of the learnings of young children are motor in character, with the child devoting a good proportion of his attention to skills of a locomotor nature. Furthermore, learnings of a motor nature tend to usurp a large amount of the young child's time and energy and are often closely associated with other learnings. In addition, it is well known by experienced classroom teachers at the primary grade levels that the child's motor mechanism is active to the extent that it is almost impossible for him to remain for a very long period of time in a quiet state regardless of the passiveness of the learning situation.

To demand prolonged sedentary states of children is actually, in a sense, in defiance of a basic physiological principle. This is concerned directly with the child's basic metabolism. The term *metabolism* is concerned with physical and chemical changes in the body which involve producing and consuming energy. The rate at which these physical and chemical processes are carried on when the individual is in a state of rest represents his basal metabolism. Thus, the basal metabolic rate is indicative of the speed at which body fuel is changed to energy, as well as how fast this energy is used.

Basal metabolic rate can be measured in terms of calories per meter of body surface, with a calorie representing a unit measure of heat energy in food. It has been found that on the average, basal metabolism rises from birth to about two or three years of age, at which time it starts to decline until between the ages of twenty to twenty-four. Also the rate is higher for boys than for girls. With the relatively highest metabolic rate and therefore the greatest amount of energy occurring during the early school years, deep consideration might well be given to learning activities through which this energy can be profitably utilized. Moreover, it has been observed that there is an increased attention span of primary-age children during active play. When a task such as a motor learning experience is meaningful to a child, he can spend longer periods engaged in it than is likely to be the case in some of the more traditional types of learning activities.

The comments made thus far have alluded to some of the general aspects of the value of the motor activity learning medium. The ensuing discussions will focus more specifically upon what we call certain inherent facilitative factors in this approach which are highly compatible with child learning. These factors are motivation, proprioception, and reinforcement, all of which are somewhat interdependent and interrelated.

Motivation

In consideration of motivation as an inherent facilitative factor of learning through motor activity, we would like to think of the term as it is described in the *Dictionary of Education.* That is "the practical art of applying incentives and arousing interest for the purpose of causing a pupil to perform in a desired way." (11)

11. Good, p. 354.

We need also to take into account both extrinsic and intrinsic motivation. Extrinsic motivation is described as "appreciation of incentives that are external to a given activity to make work palatable and to facilitate performance," while intrinsic motivation is the "determination of behavior that is resident within an activity and that sustains it, as with autonomous acts and interests." (12)

Extrinsic motivation has been and continues to be used as a means of spurring individuals to achievement. This most often takes the form of various kinds of reward incentives. The main objection to this type of motivation is that it tends to focus the learner's attention upon the reward rather than the learning task and the total learning situation.

In general, the child is motivated when he discovers what seems to him to be a suitable reason for engaging in a certain activity. The most valid reason, of course, is that he sees a purpose for the activity and derives enjoyment from it. The child must feel that what he is doing is important and purposeful. When this occurs and the child gets the impression that he is being successful in a group situation, the motivation is intrinsic, since it comes about naturally as a result of the child's interest in the activity. It is the premise here that the motor activity learning medium contains this built in ingredient so necessary to desirable and worthwhile learning.

The ensuing discussions of this section of the chapter will be concerned with three aspects of motivation that are considered to be inherent in the motor activity learning medium. These are 1) motivation in relation to interest, 2) motivation in relation to knowledge of results, and 3) motivation in relation to competition.

Motivation in Relation to Interest

It is important to have an understanding of the meaning of interest as well as an appreciation of how interests function as an adjunct to learning. As far as the meaning of the term is concerned, the following description given some time ago by Lee and Lee expresses in a relatively simple manner what is meant by

12. *Ibid.*

the terms *interest* and *interests:* "Interest is a state of being, a way of reacting to a certain situation. Interests are those fields or areas to which a child reacts with interest consistently over an extended period of time." (13)

A good condition for learning is a situation in which a child agrees with and acts upon the learnings which he considers of most value to him. This means that the child accepts as most valuable those things that are of greatest interest to him. To the very large majority of children, their active play experiences are of the greatest personal value to them.

Under most circumstances a very high interest level is concomitant with pleasurable physical activities simply because of the expectations of pleasure children tend to associate with such activities. The structure of a learning activity is directly related to the length of time the learning act can be tolerated by the learner without loss of interest. These kinds of experiences by their very nature are more likely to be so structured than many of the traditional learning activities.

Motivation in Relation to Knowledge of Results

Knowledge of results is most commonly referred to as feedback. It was suggested by Brown many years ago that feedback is the process of providing the learner with information as to how accurate his reactions were. (14) Ammons has referred to feedback as knowledge of various kinds which the performer received about his performance. (15)

It has been reported by Bilodeau and Bilodeau that knowledge of results is the strongest, most important variable controlling performance and learning, and further that studies have repeatedly shown that there is no improvement without it, progressive

13. J. Murray and Dorris May Lee, *The Child and His Development* (New York, Appleton-Century-Crofts, 1958), p. 382.

14. J. S. Brown, A Proposed Program of Research on Psychological Feedback (Knowledge of Results) in the Performance of Psychomotor Tasks, Research Planning Conference on Perceptual and Motor Skills, AFHRRC Conf. Rept. 1949, (U.S. Air Force, San Antonio, Texas), pp. 1-98.

15. R. B. Ammons, "Effects of Knowledge of Performance: A Survey and Tentative Formulation," *Journal of General Psychology,* Vol. LIV, (1931), pp. 279-99.

improvement with it, and deterioration after its withdrawal. (16) As a matter of fact, there appears to be a sufficient abundance of objective evidence that indicates that learning is usually more effective when one receives some immediate information on how he is progressing. It would appear rather obvious that such knowledge of results is an important adjunct to learning because, without it, one would have little idea of which of his responses were correct.

The motor activity learning medium provides almost instantaneous knowledge of results because the child can actually see and feel himself throw a ball, or tag, or be tagged in a game. He does not become the victim of a feedback mechanism in the form of a poorly constructed paper-and-pencil test, the results of which may have little or no meaning for him.

Motivation in Relation to Competition

Using games as an example to discuss the motivational factor of competition, we will describe games as active interactions of children in cooperative and/or competitive situations. It is possible to have both cooperation and competition functioning at the same time, as in the case of team games. While one team is competing against the other, there is cooperation within each group. In this framework it could be said that a child is learning to cooperate while competing. It is also possible to have one group competing against another without cooperation within the group, as in the case of games where all children run for a goal line independently and on their own.

The terms *cooperation* and *competition* are antonymous; therefore, the reconciliation of children's competitive needs and cooperative needs is not an easy matter. In a sense, we are confronted with an ambivalent condition, which if not carefully handled could place children in a state of conflict.

Modern society not only rewards one kind of behavior (cooperation) but its direct opposite (competition). Perhaps more often than not our cultural demands sanction these rewards

16. Edward A. and Ina Bilodeau, "Motor Skill Learning," *Annual Review of Psychology* (Palo Alto, California, 1961), pp. 243-270.

without provision of clear-cut standards with regard to specific conditions under which these forms of behavior might well be practiced. Hence, the child is placed in somewhat of a quandary with reference to when to compete and when to cooperate.

As far as the competitive aspects of some motor activities, such as active games are concerned, they not only appear to be a good medium for learning because of the intrinsic motivation inherent in them, but this medium of learning can also provide for competitive needs of children in a pleasurable and enjoyable way.

Proprioception

Earlier in this chapter it was stated that the theory of learning accepted here is that learning takes place in terms of a reorganization of the systems of perception into a functional and integrated whole as a result of certain stimuli. These systems of perception, or sensory processes as they are sometimes referred to, are ordinarily considered to consist of the senses of sight, hearing, touch, smell, and taste. Armington has suggested that "although this point of view is convenient for some purposes, it greatly over-simplifies the ways by which information can be fed into the human organism." (17) He indicates also that a number of sources of sensory input are overlooked, particularly the senses that enable the body to maintain its correct posture. As a matter of fact, the sixty to seventy pounds of muscle, which include over six hundred in number, that are attached to the skeleton of the averaged-sized man could well be his most important sense organ.

Various estimates indicate that the visual sense brings us upwards of three-fourths of our knowledge. Therefore it could be said with little reservation that man is *eye-minded.* However, Steinhaus has reported that "a larger portion of the nervous system is devoted to receiving and integrating sensory input originating in the muscles and joint structures than is devoted to the eye and ear combined." (18) In view of this, Steinhaus has contended that man is *muscle sense* minded.

17. John C. Armington, *Physiological Basis for Psychology* (Dubuque, Iowa, Wm. C. Brown Co., Publisher, 1966), p. 16.
18. Arthur H Steinhaus, "Your Muscles See More Than Your Eyes," *Journal of Health, Physical Education and Recreation* (September 1966).

Generally speaking, *proprioception* is concerned with muscle sense. The proprioceptors are sensory nerve terminals that give information concerning movements and position of the body. A proprioceptive feedback mechanism is involved which in a sense regulates movement. In view of the fact that children are so movement oriented, it appears reasonable to speculate that proprioceptive feedback from the receptors of muscles, skin, and joints contributes in a facilitative manner when the motor activity learning medium is used to develop science concepts. The combination of the psychological factor of motivation and the physiological factor of proprioception inherent in the motor activity learning medium has caused us to coin the term mot*or*vation to describe this phenomenon.

Reinforcement

In considering the compatibility of the motor activity learning medium with reinforcement theory, the meaning of reinforcement needs to be taken into account. An acceptable general description of reinforcement would be that there is an increase in the efficiency of a response to a stimulus brought about by the concurrent action of another stimulus. The basis for contending that the motor activity learning medium is consistent with general reinforcement theory is that this medium reinforces attention to the learning task and learning behavior. It keeps children involved in the learning activity, which is perhaps the major area of application for reinforcement procedures. Moreover, there is perhaps little in the way of human behavior that is not reinforced, or at least reinforcible, by feedback of some sort, and the importance of proprioceptive feedback has already been discussed in this particular connection.

In summarizing this discussion, it would appear that the motor activity learning medium generally establishes a more effective situation for learning reinforcement for the following reasons:

1. The greater motivation of the children in the motor activity learning situation involves accentuation of those behaviors directly pertinent to their learning activities, making these salient for the purpose of reinforcement.

2. The proprioceptive emphasis in the motor activity learning medium involves a greater number of *responses* associated with and conditioned to learning stimuli.

3. The gratifying aspects of the motor activity learning situations provide a generalized situation of *reinforcers.*

CURRENT STATUS AND FUTURE PROSPECTS OF THE MOTOR ACTIVITY LEARNING MEDIUM

One of the reasons given for studying the history of a subject is that it helps to determine how the past has challenged the present, so that we might better understand how the present might challenge the future. As far back as the early Greeks, it was suggested by Plato that learning takes place better through play and play situations. Similar pronouncements over the years include those made by Aristotle, Quintillian, Rousseau, Froebel, and Dewey. Despite many esteemed endorsements of the motor activity approach to learning, there is not a great deal of historical evidence that indicates that there was widespread practice of it in the schools. Pestalozzi, the noted Swiss educator, who is sometimes credited with laying the foundation for modern teaching, was an exponent of the idea in his own school. As mentioned previously, Friedrich Froebel, who is considered the founder of the kindergarten, incorporated the practice as a part of the school day. Perhaps, having been influenced by some of his predecessors, John Dewey indicated his thoughts on the matter in 1919 with reference to this approach to learning in the actual school situation. He commented that "Experience has shown that when children have a chance at physical activities which bring their natural impulses into play, going to school is a joy, management is less of a burden, and learning is easier." (19)

In more recent times the use of motor activity learning in education has been given considerable attention. A concrete example of this is a statement made in the publication *The Shape of Education for 1966-67.* In a chapter entitled "Learning is Child's Play," referring to games in education, the following

19. John Dewey, *Democracy in Education, An Introduction to the Philosophy of Education* (New York, The MacMillan Co., 1919), pp. 228-229.

comment was made: "And the University of Maryland has a professor of physical education and health, James H. Humphrey, who has devised a whole series of playground games teaching the elements of language, science, arithmetic and such matters to elementary school children." Further, "The strange thing about all these incidents is that they are isolated and unrelated but that they demonstrate an educational trend for which there is respectable theoretical justification in serious academic research." (20)

It seems worthy of mention that in contemporary society there is a certain degree of universality in the use of motor activity for learning. While the ideologies of the Eastern and Western worlds may differ in many respects, apparently there is some agreement about this approach to learning. For example, Edward Hunter reports the following in his book *Brain-Washing in Red China:*

> There was even an arithmetic game in which there were two teams of fifteen players each and an umpire. Ten students on each side would represent a number from one to ten, and the other five players would represent the symbols used in arithmetic; plus (+); division (÷); multiplication (x); and equals (=). The umpire would shout out an example such as two times four minus eight equals zero, and each side would rush to line up in this order. The team to do so first was the winner. (21)

In a somewhat similar frame of reference, the Russian Ivanitchkii, has stated, "Teachers of mathematics and physics should use examples of sports in solving problems." (22)

Up to this point, we have only been extolling the rectitude of the motor activity approach to learning. Certainly we would be remiss if we did not call attention to some of its possible limitations. However, the suggested limitations of it are likely to

20. Editors of *EDUCATION U.S.A., The Shape of Education for 1966-67* (Washington, D.C., National School Public Relations Association, 1966), p. 49.
21. Edward Hunter, *Brain-Washing in Red China* (New York, The Vanguard Press, 1951), p. 46.
22. M. F. Ivanitchkii, "Physical Education of School Children – The Constant Concern of All Pedagogical Collectives," *Theory and Practice of Physical Culture,* Vol. 4 (Russian, 1962), p. 10. From an abstract by Michael Yessis, *Research Quarterly,* Vol. 35 (1964), p. 339.

center around inertia of individuals and tradition rather than the validity of the medium itself. In any event, some people in education may feel that pupils will not take the approach seriously enough as a way of learning and therefore will not concentrate on the skill or concept being taught. However, our personal experience with this medium has been quite the contrary. In another sense, some may fear that this medium of learning may be *too* attractive to children. For example, in many of our experiments in the use of this approach in the area of science many children have asked, "Why don't we learn it this way all the time?"

It should be pointed out very forcefully here that we do not necessarily recommend that learning through motor activity be the tail that wags the educational dog. But, rather we would like to look upon it as *another* valid way that children might learn and not necessarily the only way. We are well aware of the fact that everything cannot be taught best through motor activity, simply because all children do not learn in the same way.

Although it is difficult to predict what the future holds for this medium of learning, we feel pretty well assured that more serious attention is currently being paid to it. Discussions with leading neurophysiologists, learning theorists, child development specialists, and others reveal a positive attitude toward the motor activity learning medium. And there is pretty general agreement that the premise is very sound from all standpoints: philosophical, physiological, and psychological.

GENERAL WAYS OF PROVIDING SCIENCE LEARNING EXPERIENCES THROUGH MOTOR ACTIVITY

VARIOUS educators have recognized the need for children to get actively involved in science learning experiences. Misner, Schneider and Keith have suggested that, "A science curriculum should involve many experiences and demonstrations which children may observe, and in which they may participate." (23) Cramer and Domian have indicated that "Effort should be made to use actual experiences with more doing on the part of children and less reading and hearing of science." (24)

The opportunities for science experiences through motor activity are so numerous that it should be difficult to visualize a motor oriented experience, i.e. a physical education experience that is not related to science in some way. Indeed the possibilities for a better understanding of science and the application of science principles in motor activities are almost unlimited. Yet many classroom teachers, and some physical education specialists as well, for that matter, are oblivious to many of these possibilities. Indicative of this paradoxical situation is the following anecdote related by Herrick many years ago.

> One cold day when the sixth graders came in from an outdoor play period several children were discussing what could be the matter with their large rubber and soccer balls. When they took them from the cupboard they seemed to be "blown up hard enough" but after being used on the playground for a short period of time they were too soft. The teacher ended the conversation by saying, "Play period is over.

23. Paul J. Misner, Frederick W. Schneider, and Lowell G. Keith, *Elementary School Administration* (Columbus, Ohio, Charles E. Merrill Books, Inc., 1963), p. 135.
24. Roscoe V. Cramer and Otto E. Domian, *Administration and Supervision in Elementary School* (New York, Harper and Row Publishers, 1960), p. 485.

Put the balls away and get ready for science class. We are starting our
unit on air today." (25)

We would certainly like to think that this is the exception, but it
has been our observation that many such incidences as the above
prevail.

If children are to be provided with learning experiences in
science that involve the study of problems that are of real concern
in their lives, teachers might well be on the alert for those things
of interest to pupils in the daily school situation.

Although the main purpose of this text is to deal with more or
less specific ways to learn about science through motor activity,
some mention should be made about how this can occur generally.
It is the purpose of the present chapter to give consideration to
this.

The following generalized list is submitted to give the reader an
idea of some of the possible ways in which opportunities for
science experiences might be utilized through various kinds of
motor activities.

1. The physical principle of equilibrium or state of balance is
one that is involved in many motor activities. This is particularly
true of stunt activities in which balance is so important to
proficient performance.

2. Motion is obviously the basis for almost all motor activities.
Consequently, there is opportunity to relate the laws of motion, at
least in an elementary way, to movement experiences of children.

3. Children may perhaps understand better the application of
force when it is thought of in terms of hitting a ball with a bat or
in tussling with an opponent in a combative stunt.

4. Friction may be better understood by the use of a
rubber-soled gym shoe on a hard-surfaced playing area.

5. Throwing or batting a ball against the wind can show how air
friction reduces the speed of flying objects.

6. Accompaniment for rhythmic activities, such as the drum,
piano, and recordings, help children to learn that sounds differ
from one another in pitch, volume, and quality.

7. The fact that force of gravitation tends to pull heavier-than-

25. Virgil E. Herrick, *Issues in Elementary Education* (Minneapolis, Burgess Publishing
Company, 1952), p. 155.

air objects earthward may be better understood when the child finds that he must aim above a target at certain distances.

8. Ball bouncing presents a desirable opportunity for a better understanding of air pressure.

9. Weather might be better understood on those days when it is too inclement to go outside to the activity area. In this same connection, weather and climate can be considered with regard to the various sport seasons, i.e. baseball in spring and summer and games that are suited to winter play and cold climates.

It should be understood that this is just a partial list of such possibilities and a person with just a little ingenuity could expand it to much greater length.

SIMULATED TEACHING-LEARNING SITUATIONS

Over a period of time a large number of teaching-learning situations involving the learning of science through motor activity have been developed. This has been done by tape recording of dialogue between teachers and children in given situations. This material can be used to great advantage by teachers as an evaluative technique to help determine the success of this kind of procedure. Following are some representative examples of such teaching-learning situations.

One of the important objectives of science education in the elementary school is the development of a scientific attitude. The following procedure illustrates how the game *Find the Leader* could be used as a help toward understanding the meaning and importance of a scientific attitude.

TEACHER: Boys and girls, we have a new game to learn today. I think that this game will help you with something that we are trying very hard to develop this year, that is, a scientific attitude. Do you remember some of the things we have said one needs in order to have a scientific attitude?

PUPIL: One thing was getting exact information.

TEACHER: Yes, Frances, anything else?

PUPIL: Observing carefully was one.

TEACHER: Good, Bill, and anything else?

PUPIL: Learning to solve problems was one, I think.

TEACHER: That's right, John. Now this game, like so many other games, gives us a problem to solve. Also, in order to solve it, we have to observe very carefully and draw the right conclusions. Let's form a circle around the room. Leave room between your desks and the walls so you can move around a little. We will ask Larry to be the observer. When we are ready to play, Larry will go outside the room and we will choose a leader. The leader starts a motion of some kind, such as skipping, hopping, jumping, or moving some part of the body. Everyone else must do the same thing the leader does. The observer is called back into the room and he tries to find out who the leader is by watching all persons very closely. The leader will change the action frequently, but he must try to make the change while the observer is looking at someone else so as to keep the observer from finding out he is the leader. The observer is given three guesses. If he guesses the leader, he is allowed to choose the next observer. If he does not guess correctly, the leader becomes the observer. Does this game remind you of other games you have played?

PUPIL: It's a little like Follow the Leader.

TEACHER: Yes, it is something like Follow the Leader. Now, from what you know about the game so far, what are some of the things you can think of already that will help us in playing the game?

PUPIL: You shouldn't look at the leader too long or you will give him away.

TEACHER: All right. (Writes this on board)

PUPIL: The leader should change often.

TEACHER: (Writing this on board) Yes, this is important to keep the game interesting. These are good suggestions which should help us in playing the game. All right, Larry is the observer. We will also need a leader. Larry, if you will go outside, we will choose a leader. (Observer goes outside the room.) Keith has not been chosen to lead a game for some time, so suppose we have him lead. Who would like to be the messenger? All right, Freddie, you may be the messenger. Will you please tell Larry we are ready for him?

(The pupils participate in the game for a time and then the teacher evaluates it with them.)

TEACHER: Boys and girls, you did very well with this new game and it is easy to see that you enjoyed it. Can anyone think of something we could do to make it a better game?

PUPIL: It was too easy for the observer to catch the leader, because he made such big changes.

TEACHER: All right. Maybe the leader could make a little change each time instead of a big change.

PUPIL: We looked at the leader too much and the observer could tell by watching us.

TEACHER: Yes, we could probably improve on that as we get more practice. What do we have to know to play this game, particularly in terms of the scientific attitude?

PUPIL: How to be good observers.

PUPIL: How to follow the leader and change actions quickly.

PUPIL: And how to judge the best time for changing actions if you are the leader.

TEACHER: Yes, those things are very important. Do you think you improved any particular ability?

PUPIL: You have to be good at observing.

PUPIL: You have to think.

PUPIL: I was able to change from one thing to another quickly.

TEACHER: Very good. So you see that the scientific attitude is very important in games as well as in other situations.

The next procedure shows how the study of kinds of birds, their nesting habits, and their protective nature toward their young might be accomplished with a group of young children through the game of *Bird Catcher*.

TEACHER: Boys and girls, can you tell me the names of some birds that you often see around your home and around school?

PUPIL: Robins.

PUPIL: I saw a bluejay the other day. (As various names of birds are given, the teacher writes them on the board as the children say them.)

TEACHER: Yes, that's very good. You have seen many different kinds of birds. Now we have talked about the way some of these birds lay their eggs, and how the mother bird sits on them for two weeks. And then the little birds hatch just as our chicken did. What does the mother robin do for her little ones when they are hatched?

PUPIL: She feeds them.

PUPIL: She keeps them warm and protects them from harm.

TEACHER: Yes. She wants them safely in the nest, where she can protect them until they are old enough to take care of themselves. How many of you saw *Wonderful World of Disney* last week when the picture of *Waters Birds* was shown? (Several hands go up and children indicate verbally that they saw the picture.)

TEACHER: Did you see the picture of the little baby tern that wandered away from from the nest?

PUPIL: Yes, and his mother got scared.

TEACHER: Indeed she did because she saw danger for the baby. Do you remember what the mother and father tern did? George?

PUPIL: The father sat on the nest while the mother bird went to find the baby bird.

PUPIL: The mother brought it back to the nest.

TEACHER: Yes, you remember the picture very well. Now today we are going outside to play a game about birds in the nest. The name of the game is Bird Catcher. We need some robins, bluejays, etc. (The teacher uses names that were given by the children and written on the board.)

TEACHER: We also need a mother bird and a bird catcher and I want you to select two members of the class for these parts in the game. Our room is shaped like this. (The teacher makes a sketch on the board while she tells where the nest, cage, forest, etc. will be located. Following this she explains the entire game to the children, using the illustration on the board.

TEACHER: Now I want you to listen closely as I tell you how the game is played. Remember as much of it as you can. A mother bird stands in the nest. A bird catcher stands between the nest and the cage about here. (Indicates on board.) The rest of you who are in the forest will have the names of the different birds we talked about. The mother bird calls "Robins," and all of the robins run from the forest to the nest while the bird catcher tries to catch them. If he tags a robin, he takes him to the cage. All robins who reach the mother bird are safe. The mother bird calls another group of birds and the game goes on until all the birds are in the nest or the cage. The winning group is the one that has the largest number of birds safe in the nest. Now we will go out to the playground and I want you to try to play the game from our discussion here. I will give you help if you need it.

(The game is organized by the children with the assistance of the teacher. They play for a time and she evaluates it with them when they get back to the room.)

TEACHER: Now let us review what we learned today. What were some of the things we learned?

PUPIL: Names of birds.

PUPIL: The mother bird protects her babies.

TEACHER: Good, Mary, anything else?

PUPIL: The little birds should come when the mother calls them.

PUPIL: If you don't run to the nest, you will get caught.

TEACHER: Did the game do anything for our bodies?

PUPIL: It gave us exercise.

PUPIL: I like to run and be chased by the bird catcher.

TEACHER: Did you find that you had to be a good dodger to keep from being tagged? Paul?

PUPIL: Yes, and I didn't get tagged today.

TEACHER: Can you think of any ways in which we might

improve the game if we were to play it again?

PUPIL: You should run right away when your name is called.

TEACHER: Yes, anything else?

PUPIL: Don't all stick together to run because more get tagged that way.

PUPIL: Don't always run in a straight line for the nest.

TEACHER: Yes, those are all good suggestions. We should remember them when we play the game again.

The final procedure illustrates how the study of directions, under the general topical area of *The Universe* can be integrated with a game called *Weathervane.*

TEACHER: We are going to learn a new game today. I think it will help you to understand better the picture on page 163 in your *Find New Neighbors Reader.* Remember, the story was "He Who Thinks Well and Runs Quickly." Does anyone remember what the picture shows?

PUPIL: They were herding buffaloes.

TEACHER: Yes, the picture shows the buffaloes being herded from east to west. I wonder how the Indians knew which was east and west?

PUPIL: I know. They could tell by the sun.

TEACHER: Yes, they could tell by the sun. It rises in the east and sets in the west. Could any of you tell which direction was north if you knew where east or west was?

PUPIL: I think the directions always go around the same way.

TEACHER: Very good. Elsie. Then it would look something like this. (The teacher writes north, east, south and west on the board.)

TEACHER: Can you tell us on which side of our building the sun rises?

PUPIL: On this side.

TEACHER: How did you know, Fred?

PUPIL: Because the sun shines in the room in the morning.

TEACHER: Good. That would mean our room is on what side of the building?

PUPIL: I guess the east side.

TEACHER: Yes, and why?

PUPIL: You said the sun rises in the east.

TEACHER: Now I wonder if anyone can tell us which direction is north?

PUPIL: That way.

TEACHER: Fine. Now, Clinton, since you were able to tell us how we could find our directions, will you go to the table at the north end of the room and get four cards I have put there? You and Charles may place the cards on the walls in the proper directions. (While the cards are being placed, the following discussion takes place.)

TEACHER: Many people need to know directions. Can you think of anyone we have been studying about lately who would need to know directions even more than we would?

PUPIL: Pilots.

TEACHER: That's right, Danny. Anyone else?

PUPIL: Navigators on boats and automobile drivers.

TEACHER: Yes, indeed they do. Now, our cards are up. Let's check to see if they are right. Charles and Clinton have placed them correctly. Now everybody stand. I will be the weatherman for awhile and you will be the weathervanes.

PUPIL: What is a weathervane?

TEACHER: Jean was absent yesterday. Can anyone tell her?

PUPIL: It is something that you see on a building and it turns with the wind and shows the direction of the wind.

TEACHER: Now we are going to see how well you know your directions. When I say, "South," you quickly make a jump turn to the south. Now, for practice, let's try some more directions. Does everyone understand? We will work in teams. Each row is a team. If you jump the wrong way, you will know it because most of you will probably jump in the right direction. The last one in each row can count how many jumped the wrong way and each one will be a point against your team. (The game proceeds for a short time and the teacher asks how it might be played differently.)

TEACHER: What is another way that we could play this game?

PUPIL: Instead of jumping we could hop on one foot in the direction.

TEACHER: Shall we try that?

(The game is played in this manner for a short time.)

TEACHER: Are there any other ways we could play the game?

PUPIL: We could make a relay out of it like when we had classroom relays during our last physical education period.

TEACHER: Do you have suggestions as to how we might do this, Don?

PUPIL: You could draw a square in front of each row and write the directions on the sides of each square. We could run up and put a piece of chalk in the place the way the directions go.

(The relay is organized with the help of the teacher. At the end of the period the teacher evaluates with the class.)

TEACHER: What were some of the things we learned by playing this game?

PUPIL: You can tell the east and west by the sun.

PUPIL: The sun rises in the east.

PUPIL: The sun sets in the west.

TEACHER: Yes, and we also found that north, east, south and west follow in clockwise rotation. What is opposite north?

PUPILS: South.

TEACHER: What is opposite west?

PUPILS: East.

TEACHER: Do you understand the picture in your reader better?

PUPIL: Yes, I'll look for the sun in pictures now.

TEACHER: How does the sun help pilots and navigators?

PUPIL: They can tell directions from it.

PUPIL: I know another way we could play, by using northeast and southeast.

TEACHER: That sounds like a good idea, Ronald. Suppose you and some of the other boys show us another way to play, using more directions. Maybe we can try it next time.

The illustrations that have been presented here should give some idea of how learning of science concepts can take place in actual teaching-learning situations. Perhaps these illustrations could serve as a guide for teachers in planning their own lessons.

DEVELOPING SCIENCE CONCEPTS THROUGH MOTOR ACTIVITY IN BROAD UNITS OF STUDY

Another general way in which science learning through motor activity can take place is by utilizing such learning activities in broad units of study. It will be the purpose of the final section of this chapter to illustrate some of these possibilities.

When the history of education is considered over a period of several hundred years, the unit may be thought of as a more or less recent innovation. Because of this, it is difficult to devise a universal definition for the term unit. This is due partly to the fact that the term does not at the present time have a fixed meaning in the field of education. Essentially, the purpose of unitary teaching is to provide for a union of component related parts which evolve into a systematic totality. In other words the unit should consist of a number of interrelated learnings which are concerned with a specific topic or central theme. A variety of types of experiences as well as various curriculum areas are drawn upon for the purpose of enriching the learning medium for all children so that the understandings of the topic in question can be developed.

It will not be the purpose here to consider the advantages or disadvantages of the various types of units that have been discussed in textbooks and the periodical literature. On the contrary, it will be the purpose to relate to motor activity learning through the role of physical education as a curriculum area to be "drawn upon for the purpose of enriching the learning medium for all children so that the understandings of the topic in question can be developed."

There is universal agreement among educators that the things children do — the activities — are by far the most important part of the unit. Yet those experiences through which many children tend to learn best, that is, active play experiences, have been grossly neglected as essential and important activities of the unit. There is, however, an explanation for this paradoxical phenomenon. For example, the classroom teacher, who in most cases is well prepared to guide and direct many learning experiences and activities of the unit, may not feel confident enough to include physical education activities as a means of developing the concepts of the unit. Moreover, when there is a physical education specialist available to assist the classroom teacher, this individual may not be familiar enough with the other curriculum areas to recommend physical education activities that will be of value in developing unit concepts.

It may be recalled that in Chapter One, it was stated that one of the ways of providing and organizing science learning experiences was that of incorporating science experiences in large units of study, as in the social studies.

In order to show more clearly how physical education can be used as a means of extending the basis for learning in broad units of study, a concrete example is submitted at this point. The materials presented include exerpts from social studies units that have been developed by groups of elementary school administrators and teachers under the supervision of the author. Many of the motor activities have been used with success in developing science concepts in practical teaching-learning situations.

The following example concerns a major social studies area for a particular fourth grade called "Learning About Our World." The unit is entitled "The Earth and the Sky." It is subdivided into two areas called "Exploring the Earth" and "Exploring the Sky." In this particular unit there are many concepts to be developed. It was found through experimentation that several of the concepts could be further developed through the use of a variety of motor activities. Following is a sampling of the concepts of the unit and the activities used in their development.

LEARNING ABOUT OUR WORLD

1. Exploring the Earth
   a. Concept: *The earth spins around like a top.* This concept

was further developed through a stunt called *The Top.* This is an individual activity in which the child stands with his feet close together and his arms at his sides. He jumps into the air with the use of his arms and attempts to turn completely around and land in his original position.

b. Concept: *The earth exerts a force called gravity.* This concept was further developed in discussions of those activities that involved throwing an object such as a ball into the air. (Gravity keeps a ball from continuing to go up into the air.)

c. Concept: *"Up" is away from the earth and "down" is toward the earth's center.* This concept was further developed through the activity *Up-and-Down Relay.* In this activity the class is divided into a number of equal groups and each group forms a column. All of the players stoop down in a squatting position. At a signal the last person in each column stands and taps the person in front of him on the shoulder. This person stands and taps the person in front of him on the shoulder. This procedure continues until all persons in the column are standing (up). The procedure is then reversed and the first person on the column turns and taps the person behind him on the shoulder. This person stoops down to his first position. This procedure continues until all players are in their original position (down).

d. Concept: *Places near the equator usually have hotter summers and warmer winters than those farther away from it.* This concept was further developed through a game called *Equator Hotter.* In this game the members of the class station themselves in a scattered formation within a given area. The teacher places an object (a piece of colored yarn is suitable) on the person of one of the players. The object should not be concealed but large enough so that it can be seen. All of the players except one, who is *It,* know where the object is. *It* tries to locate the object and is given clues by other members of the class. As *It* hunts for the object, the other players call out "equator" in different tones to show *It* how near or far he is from the object. For example, soft tones mean farther away and loud tones mean nearer. When *It* finds the object he calls out the person's name who has it and all other persons try to get to a previously designated safe place before being tagged by *It*. A point can be scored against all caught. The game continues with another player becoming *It*.

2. Exploring the Sky
   a. Concept: *The sun rises in the east and sets in the west.* This concept was further developed through the stunt *The Rising Sun.* This is an individual activity in which the child sits down with his knees drawn up as close as he can get them to his chest. He clasps his hands together in front of his ankles. He rocks back until his feet are in the air and then he rocks forward until his feet are in the original starting position. (The directions east and west can be indicated.)
   b. Concept: *The length of shadows on earth vary at different times during the day.* This concept was further developed through the game *Shadow Tag.* In this game the players are dispersed over the playing area, with one player designated as *It*. If he can step on or get into the shadow of another player, that player becomes *It*. A player may keep from being tagged by getting into the shade or by moving in such a way that *It* finds it difficult to step on his shadow.
   c. Concept: *Tides result from the gravitational pull of the moon and the sun on the earth.* This concept was further developed through a game called *Pull With the Tides.* In this game the group forms a circle and joins hands. A circle is drawn inside the circle of players about twelve inches in front of the feet of the players. At a signal the circle "pulls as tide." Without releasing the hands, members try to force other members into the drawn circle. When a player is forced into the drawn circle, a point is scored against him and the game continues. If any of the players release hands, a point is scored against them.
   d. Concept: *Gravity keeps the planets in their elliptical orbits.* This concept was further developed through the game *Jump the Shot.* This game is most successful when played

in small groups of from six to ten players. The players form a circle and face the center. The teacher or a child selected as the leader stands in the center of the circle. The leader holds the *shot* in his hand. The shot is a soft object, such as a bean bag or a cloth bag, filled with a soft material and tied to the end of a length of rope. The leader begins the game by swinging the shot around the circle so that it starts low and reaches a point of about twelve to fifteen inches in height. He lets out enough rope so that the shot is near the feet of the players in the circle. Those in the circle try to avoid being hit with the shot by jumping over it as the leader swings it around. If the shot touches the feet of any person in the circle while it is being swung around, a point is scored against him. The game proceeds in this manner and periodically a new leader is selected.

e. Concept: *Air gets less dense as we travel out into space away from the earth.* This concept was further developed through a game called *Thin Air.* The game is played in the same manner as Equator Hotter. When *It* gets close to the object, the players say, "The air is getting denser;" when *It* goes away from the object, the players say, "The air is getting thinner." The object may be considered as the earth and the air is most dense near the object.

Another way of providing and organizing science learning experiences suggested in Chapter One was the use of separate science units. The following example of how motor activities can be used in a separate science unit concerns a first grade unit on Simple Machines. In this case the physical education teacher became a co-worker, so to speak, of the first grade teacher. The information reported here was used in the reinforcement of science concepts through the motor activity learning medium. That is, the physical education teacher reinforced the concepts taught by the classroom teacher by having the children engage in certain activities in which the concepts were inherent. (The study will be reported in detail in the following chapter.) Some of the concepts and descriptions of the activities to reinforce the concepts follow:

1. Concept: *Air can push things.* This concept was reinforced by

an adaptation of the game *Duck, Duck, Goose.* The players sit on the surface area with legs crossed, in a single circle formation. A child selected to be *It* walks around the outside of the circle, tapping various players lightly on the head repeating with each tap, "Duck." (For this situation the word "duck" was changed to "calm.") When *It* touches a player and says, "Goose," that player must stand and run after *It.* (For this situation the word "goose" was changed to "wind.") If the Goose catches *It* they change places. If not, a new person is chosen to be *It.*

2. Concept: *Electricity makes things move.* This concept was reinforced by a game called *Pincho.* The children stand in a line formation holding hands. One child who is *It* stands about ten feet in front of and facing the line. The game begins when a player at the head of the line reacts to a visual stimulus from the teacher and calls "switch on." He then squeezes the hand of the player next to him. The line then begins to walk forward and *It* begins to walk backward keeping his distance to about ten feet. While the line is moving forward the pinch or squeeze (the current) is passed on down the line very carefully, so that *It* cannot detect any movement. When the last player in the line receives the current, he shouts "switch off," and all players drop hands and run back to the original starting line. At the same time *It* makes an attempt to tag one or more players. If desirable, some sort of scoring system can be devised.

3. Concept: *Magnets pick up iron.* This concept was reinforced by the game *Iron Tag.* Players are scattered around the activity area. Each player is a magnet. In order to be "safe" they must be in contact with a piece of metal. A child is chosen to be *It.* The teacher calls "change" and all of the players must move to a new piece of metal while *It* tries to tag one or more players. Those tagged become helpers and can tag other players. The game is ended when there is only one player remaining as a magnet.

4. Concept: *Wheels move.* This concept was reinforced by the tumbling activity the *Forward Roll.* A soft landing surface such as matting is needed for this activity. Keeping the knees

together the child squats down placing the hands outside the feet. The weight is on the toes and slightly forward. The chin is tucked down to touch the chest and the child bends down almost touching the head to the mat. The body is thrust forward from the balls of the feet with the hands on the mat landing first on the upper part of the back (not on the head) and rolling down to buttocks and feet and then to a standing position. (in performing this activity the child's body simulates a wheel.)

5. Concept: *A lever is a simple machine.* This concept was reinforced by a stunt called the *Wheelbarrow.* Two children perform this stunt. One child stretches out with his hands on the surface area with the weight on the hands and the elbows extended. The other child grasps the legs of the first child and holds them against his hips while standing between the legs. The first child walks forward on his hands with the second child holding him as a wheelbarrow. The procedure is reversed so that each has an opportunity to be the wheelbarrow.

RESEARCH IN LEARNING ABOUT
SCIENCE THROUGH MOTOR ACTIVITY

....

IT was mentioned in Chapter Two that learning through motor activity is not necessarily a recent innovation. In fact, over the years the literature on this general area has been replete with pronouncements of eminent philosophers and educators. A representative sampling of these comments follow:

Plato (380 B. C.) Lack of activity destroys the good condition of every human being, while movement and methodical physical exercise save it and preserve it.

Aristotle (350 B. C.) It should not be forgotten that it is through play that the path is opened toward occupations of later age, and it is for this reason that the majority of games are imitations of work and actions which will be used in later life.

Quintillian (100 A. D.) Play ... is a sign of vivacity, and I cannot expect that he who is always dull and spiritless will be of an eager disposition in his studies, when he is indifferent even to that excitement which is natural to his age.

Comenius (1650) Intellectual progress is conditioned at every step of bodily vigor. To attain the best results, physical exercise must accompany and condition mental training.

Rousseau (1750) If you would cultivate the intelligence of your pupil, cultivate the power that it is to govern. Give his body continual exercise; make him robust and sound in order to make him wise and reasonable.

Friedrich Froebel (1830) It is by no means, however, only the physical power that is fed and strengthened in these games; intellectual and moral power, too, is definitely and steadily gained and brought under control.

Herbert Spencer (1860) We do not yet sufficiently realize the truth that is as, in this life of ours, the physical underlies the mental.

G. Stanley Hall (1902) For the young, motor education is cardinal,

46

and is now coming in due recognition, and for all, education is incomplete without a motor side. For muscle culture develops brain centers as nothing else yet demonstrably does.

John Dewey (1919) Experience has shown that when children have a chance at physical activities which bring their natural impulses into play, going to school is a joy, management is less of a burden, and learning is easier.

L. P. Jacks (1932) The discovery of the educational possibilities of the play side of life may be counted one of the greatest discoveries of the present day.

Thus spoke some of the most profound thinkers in history. Most of them have expressed themselves in various ways as far as educational and philosophical thought is concerned. The favorable pronouncements of such people with regard to the possibilities of intellectual development through motor activity obviously carry a great deal of weight. However, in an age when so much emphasis is placed upon scientific inquiry and research, we cannot accept only the subjective opinions of even some of history's most profound thinkers; thus, there is the necessity to place an objective base under a long-held theoretical postulation.

RESEARCH TECHNIQUES

How does one go about studying the motor activity learning phenomenon to see if learning actually does take place through this medium and how well it compares with some of the traditional ways of learning?

There are a number of different ways of studying how behavioral changes take place in children. After some amount of study and experimentation a certain sequence of techniques emerged as the most appropriate way to evaluate how well children might learn through motor activity. These techniques can be generally identified as follows:

1. Naturalistic Observation
2. Single-Group Experimental Procedure
3. Parallel-Group Experimental Procedure
4. Variations of Standard Experimental Procedures

Naturalistic Observation

In our work in this area one of the first problems to be reckoned with was whether this type of learning activity could be accomplished in the regular school situation, and also whether teachers whose preparation and experience had been predominantly in traditional methods would subscribe to this particular approach. To obtain this information, a procedure that could best be described as naturalistic observation was used. This involved the teaching of a concept in science to a group of children using a motor activity in which the concept was inherent. The teacher would then evaluate how well the concept was learned through the motor activity learning medium. The teacher's criteria for evaluation were his or her past experiences with other groups of children and other learning media. Three representative *cases* of the process of naturalistic observation follow. Each contains a statement of the concept to be developed, the activity and a specific application of it, and an evaluation by the teacher.

Case 1

Concept: Each planet travels on its own path called its orbit and is held in place by the sun's gravity.

Activity: *Merry-Go-Round.* This is a group stunt in which six children lie on their backs with their feet touching in the center. Six more children take positions standing between each two children in the lying position and all grasp hands. The children who are standing walk sidewards around the circle, carrying the horizontal children around with them. The heels of the horizontal children move as they are carried around the circle.

Application: This stunt was presented when the class was studying about the sun and the planets, and it was thought that it might be a good opportunity to use it to emphasize the concept. The children first did the stunt as presented and immediately many of them were able to make the transition to using it as a demonstration of the concept. The children on the floor forming the star were the sun. Those standing and holding hands were the planets. These planets were held to their orbits by the invisible force of the sun called gravity. As they got into position, those representing the sun were told to hold on tightly and to exert a force pulling the planets toward them while the planets walked around. At a signal from a leader some of these on the outside were to be released by the sun. They were asked to break the fall with their hands. They experienced a falling away tendency which was interpreted as what might happen if the sun's gravity did not hold the planets in place.

Evaluation: The children were very interested and able to make their own deduction. Some of the more advanced ones began to see the beginnings of the concept of centrifugal force — the pull of the planets in their orbits away from the sun, and some very intelligent questions arose and beginnings of a new problem to solve. This appeared very significant to the teacher because it tended to serve as a stimulating and interesting introduction to another concept. This had not occurred in other classes when the motor activity learning medium had not been used.

Case 2

Concept: Things which are balanced have equal weights on either side of their central point.

Activity: *Rush and Tug.* This is a combative activity in which the class is divided into two groups with each group standing behind one of two parallel lines which are about forty feet apart. In the middle of these two parallel lines a rope is laid perpendicular to them. A cloth is tied in the middle of the rope to designate both halves of the rope. On a signal, members of both groups rush to their half of the rope, pick it up and tug toward the group's end line. The group pulling the mid-point of the rope past its own endline in a specified amount of time is declared the winner. If at the end of the designated time the mid-point of the rope has not been pulled beyond one group's endline, the group with the mid-point of the rope nearer to its endline is declared the winner.

Application: In performing this combative activity it was decided to have the group experiment with all kinds of combinations of teams such as boys versus boys, girls versus girls, boys versus girls, big ones against little ones, and mixed sizes and weights against the same.

Evaluation: This was a very stimulating experience for the group since it presented to them a genuine problem-solving situation in trying to get the exact combination of children for an equal balance of the two teams. When there was enough experimenting, two teams of equal proportions were assembled and it was found that it was most difficult for either to make any headway. They also discovered that an equal balance depended not only on the weight of their classmates but to some upon their strength as well. Other classes where the motor activity learning medium had not been used had shown much less interest in this important concept. It was speculated that this was perhaps due to the fact that the procedure presented problem-solving situations that were of immediate interest and concern to the children in a concrete manner.

Case 3

Concept: The lever is one of the six simple machines for performing work. There are three classes of the lever. In the third class lever, the effort is placed between the load and the fulcrum. (The forearm is a third class lever.)

Activity: *Volleyball Serve.* When serving right-handed, the ball rests on the palm of the left hand and is held near the right side of the body. The left foot is slightly in advance of the right foot and the knees should be slightly bent. The right arm is swung back and then forward, making contact with the ball that is on the left hand. After contact with the ball, the right arm is extended forward and up in a follow-through motion. The ball should be hit with the heel of the right hand.

Application: The children were told that serving is a basic skill used in the game of volleyball and that for a successful game of volleyball, it is necessary to learn to serve the ball properly. The children were divided into two groups, each group spaced in a pattern on one side of the net facing the other group. After the teacher had demonstrated the serve, each child was given several opportunities to attempt to serve the ball. Some were able to perform rather proficiently, but it was obvious that others would need more practice.

Evaluation: After the activity was over they discussed how the arms had acted as levers in this action. Since they had already talked about first-class and second-class levers, the children said they could see how the arm was like a lever also, but that it was a little different. They discussed this difference and the fact that the elbow joint was the fulcrum, the forearm the effort, and the ball was the load. This led some pupils to suggest other examples that would illustrate this type of lever, i.e. a man swinging a golf club and a boy swinging at a ball with a bat.

Naturally, this procedure is grossly lacking in objectivity because there is only a subjective evaluation of the teacher to support the hypothesis. However, in the early stages of the work, this technique served our purpose well because at that time we were mainly concerned with having teachers experiment with the idea and to ascertain their reaction to it. In a vast majority of cases the reactions of teachers were very positive.

Single Groups

The next factor that needed to be taken into consideration was whether or not children could *actually* learn through the motor activity learning medium. Although for centuries empirical evidence had placed the hypothesis in a very positive position, there was still the need for some objective evidence to support the hypothesis. In order to determine if learning could actually take place through motor activity, the single group technique was employed. This technique involved the criterion measure of objective pretesting of a group of children on certain concepts in science. Motor activities in which the science concepts were inherent were taught to the children over a specified period of time and used as learning activities to develop the skills or concepts. After the specified period of time the children were retested and served as their own controls for comparing results of the post test with the results of the pretest.

All of our studies involving this technique in which the subjects were their own controls have shown significant differences between pretest and post test scores at a very high level of probability. Therefore, it appeared reasonable to generalize that learning actually could take place through the motor activity learning medium.

Parallel Groups

With the preceding information at hand, the next and obviously the most important step in the sequence of research techniques was to attempt to determine how the motor activity learning medium compared with other more traditional media. For this purpose the parallel group technique was used. This involved pretesting children on a number of concepts in science and equating them into two groups on the basis of pretest scores. One group would be designated as the motor activity group (experimental group) and an attempt made to develop the concepts through the motor activity learning medium. The other group would be designated as the traditional group (control group) and an attempt made to develop the concepts through one or more traditional media. Both groups would be taught by the same classroom teacher over a specified period of time. At the end of the experiment both groups would be retested and comparisons made of the post test scores of both groups.

Variations of Standard Experimental Procedures

Along with the above, a number of variations of standard techniques have been employed. In studying the effectiveness of the motor activity learning medium for boys compared to girls, a procedure was used that involved parallel groups of boys and girls within the total single group.

In those cases where an attempt has been made to hold a certain specific variable constant, three groups have been used. In this situation one group becomes an observing or non-participating group.

Another variation has been to equate children into two groups with each group taught by a different teacher. This can be done for the purpose of comparing the physical education teacher, who would not likely be skilled in teaching concepts in another curriculum area, with a superior classroom teacher who would likely be highly skilled in this direction.

In our studies the experiment is usually carried on over a period of ten days. (In some cases where conditions would permit this time period has been longer.) There are ordinarily eight and sometimes as many as ten concepts involved. A ten-day period allows for two days of testing and eight days of teaching. Reliability for the objective tests has ordinarily been obtained by using a test-retest with similar groups of children. All of our experiments have been done in the actual school situation. Obviously, it would be better to carry them out over extended periods of time, but in most cases it has been impractical to do so because it usually involves some interruption in the regular school program. In addition, it should be mentioned that our studies are much more exploratory than they are definitive. And this is ordinarily the case when conducting almost any kind of research where young children are involved.

SOME REPRESENTATIVE RESEARCH FINDINGS

In the first study reported here twenty-eight fourth grade children were pretested on eight science concepts, using the single group procedure. (26) An attempt was then made to develop the concepts through the motor activity learning medium, after which the children were tested again. The test consisted of eight items, one for each concept. The results are reported on the basis of the percent of children answering each question correctly or incorrectly before and after the motor activity learning medium was used. This method of analyzing the data was used because the small number of test items did not lend itself well to a more detailed statistical analysis. The results shown in the following table indicate that in every case a greater percentage of children answered the question correctly after the motor activity learning medium was used.

TABLE I

	First Test			Second Test		
Question	Children Answering Correctly	Children Answering Incorrectly	Percent Answering Correctly	Children Answering Correctly	Children Answering Incorrectly	Percent Answering Correctly
1	8	20	23.6	19	9	67.8
2	4	24	14.3	15	13	53.5
3	4	24	14.3	20	8	71.4
4	14	14	50	24	4	85.7
5	6	22	21.1	26	2	92.8
6	4	24	14.3	24	4	85.7
7	0	28	9	28	0	100
8	4	24	14.3	24	4	85.7

26. James H. Humphrey, *Child Learning Through Elementary School Physical Education* (Dubuque, Iowa, Wm. C. Brown Co., 1966), p. 215.

The next study reported here also involved the Single Group Procedure. (27) Twenty-four sixth grade children were pretested on eight concepts that were to be developed in a unit on energy. The test consisted of forty-four test items. After the concepts were taught through the motor activity learning medium, the children were retested. The results showed a highly significant difference in the improvement of the mean score of the second test over the mean score of the first test.

The next study is one in which the Parallel Group Procedure was used. It will be noted in the following description that this study was of a much more detailed nature than the two reported previously. The purpose of this study was to compare the use of the motor activity learning medium with traditional teaching procedures in the development of selected fifth grade science concepts. (28) In this study the science concepts were equated rather than the children. The reason for this was that an experiment that involved the equating of children would have caused too much confusion in the particular school situation where the experiment was carried out.

Seventy-two fifth grade science concepts were collected from a variety of sources which included courses of study, representative fifth grade science textbooks, and a number of science concepts charts. The concepts were organized into a scale and rated by a jury of ten educators on the basis of how difficult they were to develop with an average fifth grade class. The jury consisted of five educators whose functions were of an administrative or supervisory nature and five teachers of elementary school science judged superior by their supervisors. From the twenty concepts rated the most difficult to develop with an average fifth grade class, nine were selected that possibly could have been developed through a motor learning activity as well as traditional methods. Questions testing for knowledge of these concepts were developed and checked as to validity by means of a jury appraisal technique.

27. *Ibid,* p. 216.
28. Charles F. Ison, "An Experimental Study of a Comparison of the Use Of Physical Education Activities as a Learning Medium with Traditional Procedures in the Development of Selected Fifth Grade Science Concepts" (Unpublished Master's thesis, University of Maryland, College Park, Maryland, 1961).

Nine motor learning activities were selected to use as learning activities for developing nine of the eighteen science concepts. Traditional procedures were used to teach the remaining nine concepts. The eighteen science concepts were taught in this manner by two fifth grade teachers in separate schools. One science period was used to teach each concept, and the two methods by which the concepts were developed were alternated. No significant difference was found between the post test scores of the concepts that were taught through the different methods. Significant differences were found at a high level of probability in both classes between pretest and post test scores of the concepts taught through the motor activity learning medium. This condition existed in only one of the classes taught through traditional procedures. However, it could only be concluded that both procedures provided valid learning experiences for these particular groups. A factor strongly favoring the motor activity learning medium was that the classroom teachers' preparation and experience had been with the traditional procedures rather than with the motor activity learning medium.

A follow-up of the study just reported was conducted by equating children rather than concepts. (29) A large number of fifth grade pupils were pretested, and on the basis of the test results, forty-eight of them were equated into two groups. One group was designated as the physical education group and the other the traditional group. The same teacher taught both groups the nine concepts. The traditional group was taught through such procedures as oral presentation, visual aids, class discussion and experimentation. The physical education group was taught through physical education activities in which the concepts were inherent. After instruction of both groups over a nine-day period they were retested. Comparisons of the post tests of both groups showed a statistically significant difference in mean scores of the group that learned through motor activities. It was generalized that in this experiment learning took place better through the motor activity learning medium than through the traditional procedures.

Another very important and interesting dimension of this study

29. Humphrey, p. 216-17.

involved testing all of the children a third time at an extended interval of three months after the post test was administered. In this extended interval test the children in the physical education group had a significantly higher mean score than the children in the traditional group. These results could tend to suggest that children taught through the medium of motor activity retained the information longer than those taught through the traditional procedures.

The next study involved the reinforcement or enrichment of learning of science concepts through motor activity. (30) Twenty-three first grade children were pretested on a science unit on simple machines. The children were equated into two groups on the basis of the pretest. The classroom teacher taught eight science lessons to the entire class of twenty-three children to illustrate eight first grade science concepts involving simple machines. The teacher used regular traditional teaching procedures with the class.

Immediately after each science lesson the physical education teacher took eleven of the children (experimental group) on the basis of the pretest scores and attempted to reinforce the concepts through various kinds of physical education activities. The other twelve children (control group) took part in pleasurable activities such as art work or story telling with the classroom teacher. These activities of the control group were not related to the science concepts.

After the procedure was followed for a two-week period, all of the children were retested. The result of this post test showed that the group whose learning was reinforced by the physical education teacher through motor activities was significantly greater than the group not reinforced by such procedures. In comparing each group separately as its own control, it was indicated that the group reinforced by the motor activity learning medium gained significantly at a very high level of probability, while the other group did not improve significantly. The results also showed that the reinforcement procedure was more favorable for boys than for girls at this age level.

---

30. Iris J. Prager, "The Use of Physical Education Activities in the Reinforcement of Selected First-grade Science Concepts" (Unpublished Master's thesis, University of Maryland, College Park, Maryland, 1968).

On the basis of the results of this study, the following generalizations appeared warranted:

1. The activities taught by the physical education teacher should be considered as a reinforcement aid in teaching first grade science concepts.
2. This procedure should be given consideration in developing science concepts with first grade boys because the results were so favorable to learning for boys.
3. The physical education teacher might well be considered an important consultant in the planning of certain types of learning experiences in the science curriculum.

It is interesting to note that a later replication of this study obtained essentially the same results. (31)

In the final study reported here, two groups of fifth grade children were equated on the basis of pretest scores on science concepts. (32) One group was designated as the motor activity group and the other as the traditional group. The IQ range of the motor activity group was from 74 to 89, with a mean of 85. The traditional group's IQ range was from 72 to 90, with a mean of 83. The children were tested three times. After the first test had been administered to a large group, two groups of ten each were selected. Both groups were taught the same science concepts by the same teacher, one through traditional procedures and the other through the motor activity learning medium. The teaching was over a two-week period, at which time the children were retested. Following this second test there was no formal instruction on the science concepts that were taught during this two-week period. They were tested a third time for retention at an interval of three months after the second test.

The difference in mean scores was used as the criterion for learning. When analyzed statistically, it was found that the motor activity group learned significantly more than the traditional

31. Iris J. Prager, "The Reinforcement of First-grade Science Concepts with the Use of Motor Activity Learning," *Research Abstracts* (Washington, D. C., American Association for Health, Physical Education and Recreation, 1974).
32. James H. Humphrey, The Use of Motor Activity Learning in the Development of Science Concepts with Slow Learning Fifth-grade Children," *Journal of Research in Science Teaching*, Vol. 9, No. 3 (1972).

group. Also the motor activity group showed a high level of retention for the three-month period. Although the traditional group retained what was learned, the gain in learning was minimal to begin with. (This study will be reported in greater detail in Chapter Six, "Motor Activity Learning in Science for Slow Learning Children.")

SOME GENERALIZATIONS OF THE RESEARCH FINDINGS

It should be mentioned again that the research in this general area is much more exploratory than definitive. However, it is interesting to note that no study has shown a significant difference in traditional procedures over the motor activity learning procedures.

In view of the fact that there are now some objective data to support a long-held hypothetical postulation, perhaps some generalized assumptions along with some reasonable speculations can be set forth with a degree of confidence. Obviously, the available data reported in the foregoing studies are not extensive enough to carve out a clear-cut profile with regard to learning through motor activity. However, they are suggestive enough to give rise to some interesting generalizations, which may be briefly summarized as follows:

1. In general, children tend to learn science concepts better through the motor activity learning medium than through many of the traditional media.
2. This approach, while favorable for both boys and girls, appears to be more favorable for boys.
3. The approach appears to be more favorable for children with average and below average intelligence.
4. For children with high levels of intelligence, it may be possible to introduce more advanced concepts at an earlier age through the motor activity learning medium.

It will remain the responsibility of research to provide the conclusive evidence to support these generalizations and speculations. There is hope, however, based on actual experience with this approach in the activities described throughout this text, and particularly in the final three chapters, to encourage those responsible for facilitating children learning of science concepts to use this approach and to join in collecting evidence to verify the contribution of motor activity learning to the education curriculum.

CHAPTER FIVE...

SCIENCE MOTOR ACTIVITY STORIES
....

THROUGH reading, the individual receives the thoughts and feelings of others. Thus reading is considered a receptive phase of language. In this case the word *receptive* might carry a figurative as well as a purely literal meaning. Indeed, reading has been on the receiving end of a great deal of criticism during the past few years. Perhaps more criticism has been directed at it than all of the other elementary school curriculum areas combined. Although it may be difficult to determine precisely why reading has suffered the brunt of attack, one could speculate that it might be due to the fact that, in general, most people consider reading as the real test of learning. For example, in the early stages of American education levels, were concerned with the *reader* that that child was *in*, i.e. first reader, second reader, etc.

A good bit of the controversy involving reading seems to have centered around two general areas. First, there has been criticism of the various methods of teaching reading, and second, there has been some question regarding the validity of the principles upon which these methods are based. Perhaps because of individual differences, any method used in absolute form to the exclusion of all other methods would not meet the needs of all children. Research studies have consistently indicated that the procedures, or combination of procedures employed, should be those which best meet the needs of an individual child or a particular group of children.

It is not the purpose here to extol or criticize any of the past or present methods of teaching reading. On the contrary, the discussions and accompanying illustrations in the chapter are intended to show how motor oriented reading content can be useful in developing science concepts, while at the same time improving the child's ability to read. It might be well at the outset

61

to take into account some of the prevailing ideas with reference to *integrating* science and reading.

It has been suggested by many that interest in science can provide motivation for a desire to read. The validity of this notion is inherent in the current national interest in *the right to read.* Moreover, it is common knowledge that in some elementary schools, focus has been placed on reading to the extent that teaching in other subject areas is being oriented to improvement in reading.

Another point of view tends to hold that whatever success a child has in science should be dependent upon his ability in the area of science. Some elementary school curriculum specialists have expressed it as follows:

> Without denying the heavy reliance which all intellectual activities must have upon language skills, we wish to remind you of the equally desirable goal of permitting the child who lacks language skills to find other success in the classroom. Science is one of the subjects which *can* be studied without undue emphasis upon language. In this connection, we discourage the practice of requiring the mastery of an extensive science vocabulary except that needed to communicate within the classroom. (33)

It should be pointed out that the preceding schools of thought are not necessarily diametrically opposed. Thus, there is allowance for a degree of reliance of science and reading upon each other.

MOTOR ORIENTED READING CONTENT

Basic facts about the nature of human beings serve educators today as principles of learning. One of these principles, that the child's own purposeful goals should guide his learning activities, serves as the basis for developing motor-oriented reading content materials. Generally speaking, there are two ways in which motor-oriented reading content can be developed. These are through the language experience stories of children and prepared stories.

---

33. William Vernon Hicks and others, *The New Elementary School Curriculum* (New York, Van Nostrand Reinhold Company, 1970), p. 113.

The Language Experience Stories of Children

The language experience approach (LEA) can very effectively involve children developing group or individual stories based on motor activities, such as active games, in which they have engaged. This technique involves the usual procedures of the children first discussing important aspects of their experience in order for their stories to be detailed and accurate enough so that other children could read their story and be able to participate in the motor activity. Such aspects of reading as sufficient detail and accuracy of information, plus correct sequencing of procedures involve many higher-level cognitive aspects of problem-solving.

After the discussion, the children begin to dictate their story about how to perform the stunt, do the rhythmic activity, or play the game as the case may be. This is recorded by the teacher on the chalkboard or on large chart paper. It is important that the language patterns of children be recorded intact. The teacher records the words exactly as the children dictate them but spells the words correctly. The teacher uses guided questioning to help children put in sufficient details and proper sequence in the procedures for performing the activity in their story. After the children have dictated their story, they may reread it to be sure it has enough information so others are able to perform the activity. If it is a game, the children may even play the game again to be sure they have all the necessary steps. The language experience story based on such a physically-oriented activity facilitates the concept that the printed word symbols represent not only their oral language, but also things that they do, see, feel, and think about. In addition, certain science concepts can be internalized by means of this procedure.

Once the story has been developed, the teacher prepares a copy of the story on large chart paper (if the story was originally recorded on the chalkboard) and reproduces sufficient copies for each child to keep his own copy of the story, several copies for each child (to be used later for skill development activities), and one copy for a class book of motor activities. Individual words, phrases, and sentences from the stories can be printed on oak tag strips.

The copy of the story on large chart paper is used for teacher-directed group or individual instruction for developing the following reading skills, along with science concepts:

1. Sight vocabulary (by rereading stories; visual matching of word, phrase, sentence cards; collecting words for children's word banks), certain science-connected words may be a part of the vocabulary.
2. Word attack skills and their application to context reading (by *word hunts* for words in the story that have the same word attack patterns previously learned while working with individual words in isolation). In a sense, this can involve a scientific approach.
3. Comprehension skills of vocabulary meaning, sequence, inference, and problem-solving. This can be concerned with the scientific attitude involved in problem-solving.

The children can also help to make the class book of their stories by making illustrations for the book. The book can then be bound and made available for children to read on their own by putting it in the classroom or school library. Some children might even want to make up new games and write stories about them.

An example of such an activity by which children developed their own science motor activity story took place in a first grade classroom as follows: The particular reading activity was an outgrowth of a physical education experience that the children had with ball handling activities. The teacher had asked what they had been doing in physical education, and this experience was dictated by the children and put in chart form by the teacher. As a result of this an interesting discussion developed and in an elementary way the broad concepts of *air pressure* and *force of gravity* were introduced.

Many language experience stories such as the above can be developed from participation in games, rhythmic activities, and self-testing activities that have taken place in the regular physical education classes. This of course involves some degree of cooperation between the classroom teacher and the physical education teacher. In those instances where the responsibility for teaching physical education rests with the classroom teacher, it is a relatively easy matter to integrate these experiences when it seems appropriate.

Prepared Stories

One of the early and possibly the first attempt to prepare motor-oriented reading content as conceived here is the work of the present author and one of his associates. (34) This original work involved a detailed study of reactions of six to eight-year-old children when independent reading material is oriented to active game participation. The experiment was initiated on the premise of relating reading content for children to their natural urge to play.

Ten games were written with a story setting that described how to play the games. The manuscripts were very carefully prepared. Care was given to the reading values and the literary merits of each story. Attention was focused upon: 1) particular reading skills; 2) concept development; 3) vocabulary load, that is, in terms of number, repetition and difficulty of words, and 4) length, phrasing, and number of sentences per story.

When the manuscripts were prepared, the *New Readability Formula for Grades I-III* by George D. Spache was applied to judge the reading difficulty of the material. Following this, thirty teachers in rural, suburban and city school systems working with fifty-four reading groups of children used and evaluated the stories in actual classroom situations. The children represented, to a reasonable extent, a cross-section of an average population with respect to ethnic background, socio-economic level and the like. In all, 503 children read from one to three stories for a total of 1,007 different readings.

On report sheets especially designed for the purpose, the teachers were asked to record observable evidence of certain comprehension skills being practiced by the reading groups before, during and after the children played the games they read about. The teachers were requested to make their evaluations on a comparative basis with other materials that had been read by the children. The results of these observations were as follows:

34. James H. Humphrey and Virginia D. Moore, "Improving Reading Through Physical Education," *Education* (The Reading Issue) (May, 1960).

Comprehension Skills	Percent of Groups Practicing Skills
Following Directions	91
Noting and Using Sequence of Ideas	76
Selecting Main Idea	76
Getting Facts	67
Organizing Ideas	46
Building Meaningful Vocabulary	41
Gaining Independence in Word Mastery	35

In another dimension of the study teachers were asked to rate the degree of interest of the children in the reading on an arbitrary five-point scale as follows: extreme interest, considerable interest, moderate interest, some interest, or little or no interest. The fact that there was sustained interest in the game stories is shown in the following results. (The twenty-five cases in the last two categories involved children with I.Q.'s far below normal):

Degree of Interest	Number and Percent of Cases
Extreme Interest	469-46%
Considerable Interest	242-24%
Moderate Interest	271-27%
Some Interest	22-2.7%
Little or no Interest	3- .3%

The above results become more meaningful when it is considered that many of the classroom teachers reported that untold numbers of children sit in school and read with little or no interest. This dimension of the study tended to verify that reading is an active rather than a passive process. Apparently the children had a real and genuine purpose for reading. To satisfy their natural urge to play they were interested and read to learn how to play a new game.

On the basis of the findings and the limitations involved in conducting such an experiment, the following tentative conclusions seemed warranted:

1. When a child is self-motivated and interested, he reads. In

this case the reading was done without motivating devices such as picture clues and illustrations.

2. These game stories were found to be extremely successful in stimulating interest in reading and at the same time improving the child's ability to read.

3. Because the material for these game stories was scientifically selected, prepared and tested, it is unique in the field of children's independent reading material. The outcomes were most satisfactory in terms of children's interest in reading content of this nature.

As a result of this study additional stories were written (131 in all) and developed into a series of six books for first and second grade children and published as follows: Humphrey, James H., and Moore, Virginia D. *Read and Play.* Champaign, Illinois, Garrard Publishing, 1962 and London, Frederick Muller, 1965. Another more recent version of this work appears as: Humphrey, James H., *Learning to Listen and Read Through Movement.* Deal, New Jersey, Kimbo Educational, 1974. (Several examples of Science Motor Activity Stories from this source will be given later in the chapter.)

Widespread success resulting from the use of this material inspired the development of the same general type of reading content which would also include mathematics experiences (35) which in turn inspired a great deal of experimentation with what we arbitrarily call *The Science Motor Activity Story.*

EXPERIMENTS WITH SCIENCE MOTOR ORIENTED READING CONTENT

Early attempts to develop Science Motor Activity Stories were patterned after the original procedure used in providing for motor oriented reading content. That is, several stories were written around certain kinds of motor activities, the only difference being that the content also involved reference to science experiences. These stories were tried out in a number of situations. It soon became apparent that with some children the development of science concepts in a story was too difficult. The reason for this

---

35. James H. Humphrey, "The Mathematics Motor Activity Story," *The Arithmetic Teacher* (January, 1967).

appeared to be that certain children could not handle both the task of reading while at the same time developing an understanding of the science aspect of the story. It was then decided that since listening is a first step in learning to read, auditory input should be utilized. This process involved having children listen to a story, perform the activity, and simultaneously try to develop the science concept that was inherent in the story. When it appeared desirable, this process was extended by having the children read the story after having engaged in the activity.

MATERIALS RESULTING FROM EXPERIMENTS

As mentioned previously, all of the examples presented here are taken from *Learning to Listen and Read Through Movement* by the present author. This book contains over sixty stories about such motor activities as games, rhythms and stunts. Guidelines for teachers are presented for use of the materials. The content of the stories involves various curriculum areas in different ways and the examples that follow may be said to have a science flavor.

The first example concerns the game *Shadow Tag* which is played in the following manner: The players are dispersed over the playing area with one person designated as *It*. If *It* can step on or get into the shadow of another player, that player becomes *It*. A player can keep from being tagged by getting into the shade or by moving in such a way that *It* finds it difficult to step on his shadow. The story about this game is *The Shadow Game*.

The Shadow Game

Have you ever watched shadows?
When do you see your shadow?
What can your shadow do?
Here is a game to play with shadows.
You can play it with one or more children.
You can be *It*.
Tell your friends to run around, so you
　　cannot step on their shadow.
When you step on a shadow, that child
　　becomes *It*.
You join the other players.
Could you step on someone's shadow?

In one specific situation at first grade level the story was used to introduce the concept that shadows are formed by sun shining on various objects. Following this a definition of a shadow was given. A discussion led the class to see how shadows are made as well as why they move. The class then went outside the room to the hardtop area where many kinds of shadows were observed. Since each child had a shadow it was decided to put them to use in playing the game.

In evaluating the experience, the teacher felt that the children saw how the sun causes shadows. By playing the game at different times during the day they also observed that the length of the shadow varied with the time of day. It was generalized that the story and the participation in the activity proved very good for illustrating shadows.

The next example involves the game *Catch the Cane* which is played as follows: The children stand in a line one beside the other. Each child is given a number. One child is *It* and stands in front facing the line of children. He places a stick or bat on the surface area in an upright position and balances it by putting his finger on top of it. *It* calls out one of the numbers assigned to the children in the line. At the same time he lets go of the stick. The child whose number is called dashes to get the stick before it falls to the ground. *It* dashes to the place occupied by the child whose number was called. If the child gets the stick in time, he returns to his place in the line, and *It* holds the stick again. After the children have learned the game, several lines can be formed to provide active participation for more children. The following original story was written about this game.

Wilbur Woodchuck and His Cane

Wilbur Woodchuck hurt his leg.
He needed a cane.
At last his leg got better.
He did not need his cane.
He said, "I will find some friends.
We will play with my cane."
Wilbur's friends stood in line.
Wilbur was in front of the line.

He stood the cane in front of him.
He held it with his hand.
He called a friend's name.
Wilbur let the cane fall.
His friend caught it before it hit the ground.
He took Wilbur's place.
They played for a long time.
Could you find something to use for a cane
And play this game with other children?

The story can be used to introduce a broad understanding of the force of gravity, with an application as follows: It can be pointed out that the stick in this game represents the object which is being acted upon by the force of gravity. Every time *It* lets go of the stick, the stick begins to fall to the ground. This demonstrates the concept of the force of gravity to children. They may be helped to note that they must move faster than the force of gravity in order to catch the stick before it falls to the ground.

The following illustration is concerned with a version of the game of *Keep Away*. In this particular version of it the children arrange themselves in a circle formation. One child is chosen to be *It* and he stands outside the circle. The other children pass a ball around the circle as rapidly as they can. The ball is passed from one child to another and they try to keep the ball from being touched by *It* who runs around the outside of the circle trying to do so. If *It* touches the ball, he changes places with the child who had it. If *It* is unable to touch the ball within a certain amount of time, another child can be chosen to be *It*. The story about this game follows:

The Kittens and the Ball of Yarn

Have you ever heard of kittens playing
    with a ball of yarn?
They do many things with it.
Once some kittens found a ball of yarn.
This is what they did.
They stood close together in a circle.
One kitten was outside the circle.
The kittens in the circle passed the
    ball of yarn around.

Each kitten would take it.
He would pass it to the next kitten.
They tried to pass it quickly.
Do you know what the kitten outside
    the circle tried to do?
He ran around outside the circle.
He tried to tag the ball of yarn.
Once he did tag it.
Then he changed places with the kitten who had it.
They had fun with this game.
They played for a long time.
Could you use a rubber ball instead of a ball of yarn,
    and play this game with other children?

This activity can be used with the general area of energy to introduce in an elementary way that electricity flows along metal conductors and will not flow along non-metal conductors as glass or rubber. The ball becomes the electricity and the ball passers are the conductors. *It* is a non-conductor who tries to interfere with the flow of electricity. Any time the non-conductor is successful in interfering, the current of electricity is interrupted. Children can be encouraged to find out the kinds of materials that are non-conductors and several safety practices that have been developed for those working around electricity, both in industry and around the home.

The next activity involves the broad area of chemical and physical changes or more specifically with the idea that burning is oxidation: the chemical union of a fuel with oxygen. The game is called *Dog and Cat* but for more specific purposes here, the name is changed to *Oxygen and Fuel.* It is played in the following manner:

One child is chosen to be fuel and another child is oxygen. The remaining children join hands and form a circle, with fuel in the center of the circle and oxygen on the outside of the circle. The children in the circle try to keep oxygen from getting into the circle and catching fuel. If oxygen gets in the circle, the children in the circle then let fuel out of the circle and try to keep oxygen in, but they must keep their hands joined at all times. When oxygen catches fuel the game is over, and they join the circle while two other children become oxygen and fuel. If fuel is not caught in a specified period of time, a new oxygen can be selected. The story about this game follows:

Poochie Poodle and Clarabelle Cat

Poochie Poodle is a brave little dog.
He enjoys scampering around and chasing
    other animals.
One animal he likes to chase most is
    Clarabelle Cat.
One day he was chasing Clarabelle Cat
    all around the lawn.
Some children saw Poochie chasing Clarabelle.
They wanted to help Clarabelle.
They stood in a circle and held hands.
Clarabelle Cat went in the center of the circle.
Poochie Poodle stayed outside the circle.
Poochie tried to get in the circle
    to catch Clarabelle.
The children tried to keep him out.
Soon Poochie got inside the circle.
Then the children let Clarabelle get out
    of the circle.
It was like a game.
Finally Poochie caught Clarabelle.
Then they both stood in the circle with
    the children.
One of the children said, "I will be
    Poochie Poodle."
Another child said, "I will be Clarabelle Cat."
They played the game again and again.
Would you like to choose one child to be
    Poochie Poodle and one child to be
    Clarabelle Cat and play the game?

    An application of this activity would be to have one child represent the fuel (as trees in a forest) and another the oxygen (the air). The children in the circle can be the preventers of fire. If oxygen catches fuel and ignites him by tagging him, a fire is started. Then the game is over. In this manner children can be helped to note that oxygen feeds fire and that oxygen must be kept from fires that have started in order to put them out. The children might be encouraged to think of ways that fires are smothered, depending upon the type of burning materials.

It might appear that some of the concepts inherent in the preceding stories may be too advanced for children at which the readability level of the stories is intended. However, it should be borne in mind that the concept can be introduced broadly in an elementary way, rather than in a detailed specific way. Moreover, it may be recalled that it was mentioned in the preceding chapter that our research has indicated that it is possible to introduce more advanced concepts at an earlier age through the motor activity learning medium.

As mentioned previously Science Motor Activity Stories can be written about stunts and rhythmic activities as well as games. As far as stunts are concerned, a good opportunity is offered for understanding in the broad area of variety of life. Examples are shown in the two stories that follow involving the *Camel Walk* and the *Giraffe Walk* which are concerned with understanding that animals move around in different ways.

Casper Camel

Casper Camel lives in the zoo.
He has a hump on his back.
Could you look like Casper Camel?
You will need a hump.
Try it this way.
Bend forward.
Put your hands behind your back.
Hold them together.
That will be a hump.
That will look like Casper Camel.
Could you move like Casper Camel?
Take a step.
Lift your head.
Take a step.
Lift your head.
Move like Casper Camel.

Do you think it would be fun
to walk like Casper Camel?

George Giraffe

There is a tall animal in a far away land.
He has a long neck.
His name is George Giraffe.
You could look like him if you did this.
Place your arms high over your head.
Put your hands together.
Point them to the front.
This will be his neck and head.
Now walk like George Giraffe.
This is how.
Stand on your toes.
Walk with your legs straight.
Could you walk so you would look
     like George Giraffe?

In a situation during which children are taking turns acting out their favorite stunt story, the teacher might direct the following discussion after a child's presentation of *George Giraffe*.

TEACHER: Wasn't that interesting the way Johnny showed us how George Giraffe looked? (Children's response) What do you think George Giraffe looked like from what Johnny did? (Children's response) What did Johnny do to look tall like George Giraffe? What did Johnny do to have a long neck like George Giraffe? (Children's response) Can someone else make a long neck? (Children demonstrate) What do you have to do to walk like George Giraffe? (Children's response) Is it easy to pretend to be George Giraffe? Let's try it and find out. (All children demonstrate) Did you feel awkward? (Children's response) We often say that giraffes look ungainly or awkward. Do you think these are good words to describe a giraffe? (Children's response) Can you think of other words we might use to describe a giraffe? (Children's response) Can you think of other animals that might also look ungainly

or awkward? (Children's response) That was good
Johnny. You really showed us how to look like a
giraffe. You must have read the story very carefully.
Bobby, you said you had also read the story about
George Giraffe. Why do I say "Johnny must have
read very carefully?" (Bobby's response) That's right.
It is important to use all of the information the story
gives to help you to pretend to be something. That
was fun, wasn't it? (Children's response) All right.
Now Mary is going to tell us about her story. But this
time we are going to do it differently. This time Mary
is not going to tell us the name of her story, or what
she is pretending to be. We will have to guess who or
what she is.

In this manner the group continues to share, discuss, act out
and evaluate the stories and the animal movements the children
present.

One of the most desirable media for child expression through
movement is found in rhythmic activities. One need only to look
at the functions of the human body to see the importance of
rhythm in the life of the elementary school child. The heart beats
in rhythm; the digestive processes function in rhythm; breathing is
done in rhythm. In fact, almost anything in which human beings
are involved is done in a more or less rhythmic pattern. A very
important aspect of rhythmic activities is the classification known
as creative rhythms which are particularly pertinent to our
purpose here. Two stories are presented; the first story is oriented
to the broad area of seasonal change.

Falling Leaves

Leaves fall.
They fall from the trees.
They fall to the ground.
Fall like leaves.
Down, down, down.
Down to the ground.
Quiet leaves.
Rest like leaves.
Could you dance like falling leaves?

The second story is oriented to growth generally and to plant growth specifically.

The Growing Flowers

Flowers grow.
First they are seeds.
Be a seed.
Grow like a flower.
Grow and Grow.
Keep growing
Grow tall.
Now you are a flower.
Could you grow like a flower?

STORIES PREPARED BY TEACHERS

It is highly recommended by the present author that teachers draw upon their own ingenuity and creativeness to prepare science motor oriented stories. One of the reasons for this is the great lack of published materials in this general area, at least as it is conceived here. In addition, teachers themselves can provide materials to meet the specific needs and interests of children in a given situation. Of course a serious drawback is that preparation of such materials is such a time-consuming effort that it becomes more expedient to use professionally prepared materials. Nevertheless, it has been our experience that those teachers who have the ability and have been willing to take the time, have produced amazingly creative stories using games, stunts and rhythms. In writing such stories using a motor activity setting there are several guidelines that the teacher should keep in mind. In general the new word load should be kept relatively low. There should be as much repetition of these words as possible and appropriate. Sentence length and lack of complexity in sentences should be considered in keeping the level of difficulty of material within the independent reading levels of children. This is all the more important if the teacher decides not to use auditory input before the selection is put into the hands of the children to try to read. There are numerous readability formulas that can be utilized. For primary level stories *Spache's Readability Formula* (36) and *MaGinnis' revision of Fry's Readability Graph* (37) are well suited. For upper-level stories, Fry's Readability Graph is useful.

Consideration must also be given to the reading values and literary merits of the story. Using a character or characters in a story setting helps to develop interest. The game to be used in the story should *not* be readily identifiable. When the children identify a game early in the story, there can be resulting minimum attention on the part of the children to get necessary details in order to play the game. This also may cause attention distraction from the science concepts inherent in the story. In developing a game story, therefore, it is important that the nature of the game and procedures of the game unfold gradually.

In developing a game story the equipment, playing area, and procedures should be clearly described if necessary. Physical education terminology can be used in describing the game setting. In a file, row, or column the children stand one behind the other. In a line the children stand beside each other. Basic motor skills that can be utilized in stunt and rhythmic activities as well as for games include 1) locomotor skills (walking, running, leaping, jumping, hopping, skipping, galloping, and sliding); 2) skills of propulsion (throwing and striking with underarm, sidearm and overarm swing patterns); 3) skills of retreival (catching), and 4) axial skills (such as twisting, turning and stretching).

Games should be at the developmental level of children. At the primary level games should involve a few simple rules and in some cases elementary strategies. Games that involve chasing and fleeing, and one small group against another as well as those involving the fundamental skills mentioned above are suggested. The games should be simple enough to be able to learn and they should capitalize upon the imitative and dramatic interests which are typical of this age. (This applies to stunt and rhythmic stories as well.) Children at the upper elementary level retain an interest

36. George D. Spache, *Good Books for Poor Readers* (Champaign, Illinois. Garrard Publishing Company, 1966). (The Spache Readability Formula was used with the sample stories presented in this chapter.)
37. George H. MaGinnis, "The Readability Graph and Informal Reading Inventories, *The Reading Teacher* (March, 1969).

in some of the games they played at the primary level, and some of them can be extended and made more difficult to meet the needs and interests of these older children. In addition, games may now be introduced which call for greater bodily control, finer coordination of hands, eyes, and feet, and more strength.

In developing game stories it is also important to strive for maximum activity for all children avoiding procedures which tend to eliminate players. It may be better to devise some sort of point scoring system than to eliminate a player from the activity when he is tagged in a running game or hit with the ball in a dodgeball type game.

In summary, motor-oriented reading content provides variety to the reading program and utilizes still another way of developing concepts in science. As such, it could be said that a kind of integration can be realized as far as reading and science are concerned. High interest and motivation are the results of purposeful reading and bring words and science experiences into physical reality by playing a game, performing the stunt, or responding to the rhythm.

SOME GENERAL GUIDELINES FOR THE USE OF MATERIALS

Whether the materials for Science Motor Activity Stories are prepared by the teacher or professionally prepared, there are certain generalized guidelines which might well be considered for their use. In general this centers around 1) introducing the material, and 2) independent reading and follow-up materials.

Introducing the Material

After the prepared stories have been made available for the classroom library, the teacher may introduce several stories by reading them to the children (or tape recording them) and then having the children play the game or demonstrate the stunt or rhythm. Stories developing each type of motor activity should be selected so children will understand how the stories provide details they can use to figure out how to perform a stunt or rhythmic activity or to play a game. Sample stories should also be selected to demonstrate that some stories can be acted out by an individual child and that some require several children to participate in a game or rhythmic activity. This latter aspect of science motor-oriented reading content material utilizes another basic principle of learning, that is, the child should be given the opportunity to share cooperatively in learning experiences with his classmates (under the guidance but not the control of the teacher). The point that should be emphasized here is that, although learning may be an individual matter, it is likely to take place best in a group. This is to say that children learn individually but that socialization should be retained. Moreover, sharing in group activities seems an absolute essential in educating for democracy.

After the teacher provides auditory input with a sample story the children can be asked to carry out the activity. As the children carry out the activity the teacher accepts their efforts. The teacher may provide guidance only to the extent it is necessary to help the children identify problems and provide opportunity for them to exercise judgment in solving them and obtaining the goal — playing the game or performing the stunt or rhythm — and internalizing the science concept inherent in the story. Part of the story might be reread by the teacher if the children have difficulty in understanding how to carry out the activity. The children might be encouraged to discuss ways they could help themselves remember the details of the story.

Independent Reading and Follow-Up Activities

After such an introduction to the stories some children can be encouraged to read them on their own. The teacher and children might plan several procedures for using the stories. Such activities might include the following:

1. A group of children may select and read a story for a physical education activity.
2. Individual children may select stories involving individual stunts for a physical education period.
3. After reading one of the stories an individual child may elect to act out his favorite stunt before a group of children.

(The children might be asked to guess who or what the story describes as well as the science experience that is inherent in the story.)

4. After reading one of the stories an individual child might get several other children to read the story and participate in playing the game.

5. Children might use a buddy system for reading and acting out stories.

It is likely that in most instances the teacher will need to provide the guidance to help children with an understanding of the science concept inherent in a story. However, in many cases children will be alert to this themselves.

DEVELOPING SCIENCE CONCEPTS

WITH SLOW LEARNERS THROUGH

MOTOR ACTIVITY

....

IN very recent years there has been a tremendous upsurge of interest in attempts to provide suitable science learning experiences for children who have difficulty in learning. Tangible evidence of this concern is reflected in the fact that the National Science Teachers Association at its national convention in 1973 inaugurated a session specifically oriented to this particular aspect. This session was called "Science for the Mentally Handicapped." The success of this session prompted its continuance at the national convention of 1974 and this session was called "Science in Special Education." This session involved presentations and discussions on instructional problems with emphasis on activities that are adaptable to special education situations. It was the privilege of the present author to address both of these sessions with regard to developing science concepts with slow learning children through motor activity. (38)

The rather obvious reason for this interest lies in the fact that it is the inherent right of all children to be afforded the opportunity to learn irrespective of their limitations.

The basic principle of teaching to the individual differences of the learner has led to the development of many components within the educational system. Programs and services are becoming available in school systems that reflect the needs of those with

38. James H. Humphrey, "The Use of Motor Activity in the Development of Science Concepts with Mentally Handicapped Children," *Proceedings,* Twenty First National Convention of the National Science Teachers Association (Washington, D.C., 1973).
James H. Humphrey, "Developing Science Concepts with Slow Learning Children Through Active Games," *Proceedings,* Twenty Second National Convention of the national Science Teachers Association (Washington, D.C., 1974).

widely varying abilities and interests. Programs and services are being directed to serve citizens of all ages, beginning with the nursery-kindergarten and extending to adult education classes.

Within this broad concept of educational opportunities for our nation's population, there has developed a national concern in recent years for the problems of children with learning impairment. Direct grants for research and service for these children have enabled government agencies and private foundations to work cooperatively to help our schools do a better job both in identifying these children and providing more appropriate learning environments for them. The neurologist, the physician, the psychologist, and the researcher in education are contributing new insights into working with these children.

Some of the research in ways children with mental impairment learn provides the teacher with useful guidelines. Research has been directed not only to the etiology, the nature, and the degree of learning impairment but also to the educational environment within which learning takes place for children with such impairment. It is the premise of the author that the approach to learning through active involvement of the learner is one that needs more recognition and greater emphasis in the learning environment of those children who are identified as slow learners.

WHO IS THE SLOW LEARNER?

While there has been agreement that the needs of children with learning impairments must be reflected in appropriate teaching techniques, there is an increasing awareness of the problems of identification. Too many children in our classroom have been mistaken for slow learners because of their difficulties in mastering such academic skills as reading and arithmetic. It is essential, therefore, that there be a clear understanding of basic differences among children with the slow learner syndrome but whose learning problems may be caused by factors other than subnormal intellectual functioning. With this general frame of reference in mind the subsequent discussions will focus upon slow learners classified as 1) the child with mental retardation, 2) the child with depressed potential, and 3) the child with a learning disability.

The Child With Mental Retardation

In the literature the broad generic term *mentally retarded* encompasses all degrees of mental deficit. The designation of the term *slow learner* has been given to those children who have a mild degree (along a continuum) of subnormal intellectual functioning as measured by intelligence tests. The intelligence quotients of these children fall within the range of seventy or seventy-five to ninety. This child in the classroom is making average or below average progress in the academic skills, depending where he falls along the continuum of mental retardation. He will probably demonstrate slowness in learning such academic skills as reading and possibly arithmetic. He will very likely have difficulty in the area of the more complex mental processes of defining, analyzing, and comparing. He tends to be a poor reasoner. However, he need not necessarily be equally slow in all aspects of behavior. He may be above average in social adaptability or artistic endeavors.

In respect to physical characteristics, personality, and adjustment, slow-learning children are as variable and heterogeneous as children in the average and above-average range of intellectual potential. Attributes often identified with slow learners are laziness, inattention, and short attention. However, these characteristics are likely to be eliminated when the educational environment is geared to the needs of these children and when there is appropriateness, meaningfulness, and purposefulness to the learning activity.

There is some variance in the literature as to whether these children should be identified as mentally retarded. There is general agreement that the slow learner represents a mild degree of subnormal intellectual functioning whether or not he is labeled mentally retarded. Kirk has described the characteristic educational-life patterns of those within the broad educational categories of subnormal intelligence, namely a) the slow learner, b) the educable mentally retarded, c) the trainable mentally retarded, and d) the totally dependent mentally retarded. With reference to the slow learner he states:

> The slow-learning child is not considered mentally retarded because he is capable of achieving a moderate degree of academic success even

though at a slower rate than the average child. He is educated in the regular class program without special provisions except an adaptation of the regular class program to fit his slower learning ability. At the adult level he is usually self-supporting, independent and socially adjusted. (39)

In recent years the dimension of social adaptiveness has gained as an influencing criterion for identification of the mentally retarded. Dywab discusses the criterion of social acceptance. He speaks of the growing reluctance to identify persons as mentally retarded on the basis of intellectual subnormality alone:

> Thus a man who scores sixty-five on an intelligence test and who at that same time shows himself well able to adapt to the social demands of his particular environment at home, at work, and in the community should not be considered retarded. Indeed, we now know that he is not generally so considered. (40).

It is apparent, therefore, that the slow learner with whom the teacher may be working in the classroom may have significant intellectual subnormality.

The Child With Depressed Potential

For some years it has been recognized that factors other than intellectual subnormality affected achievement in the classroom. Concern in our schools today for the disadvantaged and culturally different children is placing increased emphasis on an understanding of these factors. Several decades ago these factors were considered by Featherstone in his delineation of the term *slow learners.* (41) He differentiated the limited educational achievement of the *constitutional slow learner* with subnormal intellectual capacity from the *functional slow learner.* The latter is often mistaken by teachers for a slow learner with limited potential because he is having difficulty achieving in the classroom. He may be making limited progress in acquiring the academic skills or he

39. Samuel A. Kirk, *Educating Exceptional Children* (Boston, Houghton Mifflin Company, 1962), pp. 85-86.
40. Gunnar Dywab, "Who Are the Mentally Retarded?" *Children,* Vol. 15 (1968), p. 44.
41. W. B. Featherstone, "Teaching the Slow Learner," in Hollis L. Caswell, ed., *Practical Suggestions for Teaching,* 2d ed., No. 1 (New York, Teachers College, Columbia University, 1951), pp. 10-11.

may be a behavior problem, but his limited achievements are caused by numerous other factors that serve to depress an individual's ability to learn. Such factors may be the lack of psychosocial stimulation from limited socioeconomic environment, inadequate hearing and vision, emotional problems in relationships with family and peers, malnutrition, or poor general health. It is important to recognize that the situation is not necessarily permanent. Both educational programs and conditions affecting the child's physical, psychological, or social well-being can be improved.

The Child With a Learning Disability

A further compounding of the problem of identification of the slow learner has occurred with studies of children who do not come under the categories of the constitutional or functional slow learner but whose classroom achievement may be similar. Johnson and Myklebust warn of the imperative need for proper identification of these children: "Often the child with a learning disability is labeled slow or lazy when in reality he is neither. These labels have an adverse effect on future learning, on self-perception, and on feelings of personal worth." (42)

The research identifying learning-disability children indicates their learning has been impaired both in specific areas of verbal and/or nonverbal learning, but their *potential* for learning is categorized as normal or above. Thus, these learning-disability children fall within the ninety and above IQ range in either the verbal or the nonverbal areas. Total IQ is not used as the criterion for determining learning potential inasmuch as adequate intelligence (either verbal or nonverbal) may be obscured in cases where the total IQ falls below ninety but in which specific aspects of intelligence fall within the definition of adequate intelligence. The learning-disability child whose IQ falls below the normal range and where a learning disability is present is considered to have a multiple involvement.

In learning-disability children there are deficits in verbal and/or

42. Doris J. Johnson and Helmer R. Myklebust, *Learning Disabilities* (New York, Grune and Stratton, 1967), p. 49.

nonverbal learning. There may be impairment of expressive, receptive, or integrative functions. There is concern for deficits in the function of input and output, of sensory modalities and overloading, and of degree of impairment. The essential differences of the mentally retarded and the learning-disability child have been characterized as the following:

> One cannot deny that the neurology of learning has been disturbed in the mentally retarded, but the fundamental effect has been to reduce potential for learning in general. Though some retarded children have isolated *high* levels of function, the pattern is one of generalized inferiority; normal potential for learning is *not* assumed. In comparison, children with learning disabilities have isolated *low* levels of function. The pattern is one of generalized integrity of mental capacity; normal potential *is* assumed.(43)

Consequently, the learning-disability child shows marked differences from the child with limited potential. There are both qualitative and quantitative differences. The learning-disability child has more potential for learning. The means by which he learns are different.

While there may be some overlapping in the educational methods used with these three groups identified as slow learners, there obviously must be differentiation in educational goals and approaches for these various groups. Correct identification of the factors causing slowness in learning is essential in the teaching to the individual differences of children. The theories and practices presented in this text outline an effective approach for teachers to use in working with the child most appropriately identified as the constitutional slow learner. However, it is recognized that the active approach to learning through motor activity is also very appropriate in many situations for those children with learning problems caused by factors other than subnormal intellectual functioning.

LEARNING CHARACTERISTICS OF THE SLOW LEARNER

When considering educational processes that would provide a successful learning experience for children with limited intellectual

43. *Ibid.*, p. 55.

potential, it is necessary to examine some of their basic character-istics of learning as found from numerous studies. Slow learners appear to follow the same patterns as those who have more adequate intellectual endowment in terms of the sequence of growth and development. The basic difference is the time schedule at which these children arrive at various levels of development. Theoretically, the child with an IQ of eighty develops intellectu-ally at a rate only four-fifths that of the average child. The rate of development of these children is more closely correlated with their mental age than their chronological age.

In a summation of the research on the learning characteristics of the mentally retarded, Johnson emphasizes that they learn in the same way as normal children. The studies indicate "remarkable agreement in the results, regardless of the environment or degree of intellectual deficit." (44)

Johnson concludes:

> Although the two groups (normal and mentally handicapped) may differ significantly on such developmental factors as life age, physical and motor development, or social development, as long as they are equated for intellectual developmental levels, experiences, and previous learnings to ensure equal readiness, they should have similar patterns of learning, require the same amounts of practice, and retain equal amounts of the material learned. (45)

Differences have been found in comparison of the learning processes in arithmetic and reading of the mentally retarded and normal children. However, according to Johnson these differences are *not* attributable to ability to learn but to the influence of instructional procedures. Included among the factors affecting the learning process are the value systems of the individual and his own concept of self as a learner. These two factors must be recognized as particularly important. The reason for this is that there are so many negative psychosocial factors operating within the life space of large percentages of the mentally retarded who can maintain themselves only in a low socioeconomic environ-ment.

---

44. C. Orville Johnson, "Psychological Characteristics of the Mentally Retarded, in William M. Cruikshank, ed., *Psychology of Exceptional Children and Youth,* 2d ed. (Englewood Cliffs, Prentice-Hall, Inc., 1963), p. 457.

45. *Ibid.,* p. 461.

Kirk's studies relating to the effect of preschool education on the development of educable mentally retarded children clearly shows that school experience can make a difference on rate of development. He has indicated that:

> It would appear that although the upper limits of development for an individual are genetically or organically determined, the functional level or rate of development may be accelerated or depressed within the limits set by the organism. Somatopsychological factors and the cultural milieu (including schooling) are capable of influencing the functional level within these limits. (46)

PRINCIPLES OF LEARNING FOR SLOW LEARNERS APPLIED TO MOTOR ACTIVITY

In providing appropriate learning experiences for slow learners, it is essential to help them be successful by structuring activities to reflect the best principles of learning. Various individuals have suggested certain principles of learning that are applicable to slow learners. A list of such principles which seems useful for our purpose is one set forth by Kirk. (47) The principles are listed as follows with implications for learning through motor activity suggested by the present author:

1. Progress is from the known to the unknown, using concrete materials to foster understanding of more abstract facts.

Implication: Use of motor activity helps children act out, and see and feel the concepts being developed and thus it becomes a part of their physical reality.

2. The child is helped to transfer known abilities from one situation to another, rather than being expected to make generalizations spontaneously.

Implication: Movement-oriented experiences enable children to work out the relationship of one situation with another and to make appropriate transfer of skills and generalizations easily.

3. The teacher may use many repetitions in a variety of experiences.

Implication: Motor activities such as active games, rhythmic

---

46. Samuel A. Kirk, *op. cit.*, pp. 100-101.
47. *Ibid.*, p. 121.

activities, and stunts provide a pleasurable, highly motivating means for necessary repetition which is not objectionable to children.

4. Learning is stimulated through exciting situations.

Implication: Personal involvement, high interest, and motivation are concomitant with learning through motor activity.

5. Inhibitions are avoided by presenting one idea at a time and presenting learning situations by sequential steps.

Implications: The structure of a motor activity such as an active game in itself implies logical ordering of ideas that are dramatized through physical movement.

6. Learning is reinforced through using a variety of sensory modalities — visual, vocal, auditory, kinesthetic.

Implication: Motor learning heightens the learning act when integrated with verbal learning experiences.

Such guidelines emphasize the need for total involvement of the learner, for using the concrete experience to develop an abstract concept, and for providing for continuity and transference of one learning experience to another. A good many years ago Featherstone also stressed the need for working with the concrete:

> One of the chief reasons for emphasizing activities based upon very concrete and tangible or objective things rather than upon predominantly verbal or abstract things is that such activities usually permit more demonstrating, constructing, picturing, and dramatizing as means of communicating ideas. (48)

Such techniques are more likely to ensure successful learning for all children, regardless of intellectual potential; for slow learners they are essential. The use of motor activity to develop abstract concepts in science is, therefore, sound methodology for all learners and particularly appropriate for the slow learner.

SOME SUPPORTING EVIDENCE

It should be recalled from Chapter Four that one of the generalizations from our research findings was that "this approach appears to be more favorable for children with average and below

---
48. W. B. Featherstone, *op. cit.*, p. 66.

average intelligence." The obvious reason for this is that slower learning children deal better with concrete learning experiences than with those which are abstract. Undoubtedly, there are few if any experiences that are more concrete, as far as children are concerned, than their active play experiences. Naturalistic observations have borne this out time and again when children have commented, "I see" after having engaged in a motor activity in which a science concept is inherent.

More objective approaches than naturalistic observation have been made to test the hypothesis and one such study was reported briefly in Chapter Four. It is repeated in greater detail here because of its appropriateness to the present chapter. (49)

Two groups of fifth grade children were equated on the basis of pretest scores on science concepts. One group was designated as the motor activity group and the other as the traditional group. The IQ range of the motor activity group was seventy-four to eighty-nine, with a mean of eighty-five. The traditional group's IQ range was from seventy-two to ninety, with a mean of eighty-three. The children were tested three times. After the first test had been administered to a large group, two groups of ten each were selected. Both groups were taught the same science concepts by the same classroom teacher, one through traditional procedures and the other through the motor activity learning medium. The teaching was over a two-week period at which time the children were retested. Following this second test there was no formal instruction on the science concepts that were taught during this two-week period. They were tested a third time at an interval of three months after the second test. The following arrays of scores show the results of all three tests for all children.

The difference in mean scores was used as the criterion for learning. When analyzed statistically, it was found that the motor activity group learned significantly more than the traditional group. Also the motor activity group showed a high level of retention for the three-month period. Although the traditional group retained what was learned, the gain in learning was minimal

49. James H. Humphrey, The Use of Motor Activity Learning in the Development of Science Concepts with Slow Learning Fifth-grade Children," *Journal of Research in Science Teaching,* Vol. 9, No. 3 (1972).

Conventional Group				Motor Activity Group			
Pupil	Test 1	Test 2	Test 3	Pupil	Test 1	Test 2	Test 3
A	43	23	40	A	43	73	73
B	23	43	43	B	23	60	67
C	37	33	37	C	37	63	73
D	50	63	60	D	50	73	90
E	53	63	50	E	53	73	83
F	47	57	60	F	47	60	70
G	47	47	53	G	47	77	63
H	33	53	40	H	33	60	67
I	50	77	63	I	50	90	87
J	33	43	57	J	33	70	60
Total	416	502	503	Total	416	699	733
Mean	41.6	50.2	50.3	Mean	41.6	69.9	73.3

to begin with.

In addition to the quantitative data reported above, there was observable evidence of many more opportunities for reasoning and problem-solving in the experiences of the motor activity group than for the group taught by traditional procedures.

In summary, on the basis of experience along with some objective evidence, it appears that the motor activity learning medium holds considerable promise for the development of science concepts for the child who has not been effectively reached by traditional methods.

CHAPTER SEVEN..

LEARNING ABOUT THE UNIVERSE AND
EARTH THROUGH MOTOR ACTIVITY

....

THE following is a summary of the motor activities in this chapter that contain science concepts in the broad area of the *Universe and Earth*. Descriptions of the activities as well as an application of each follows the summary.

Concept	*Activity*
Planet's Orbits Around the Sun	Planet Ball
Earth's Orbit Around the Sun	Earth's Orbit Relay
	Shadow Tag
	Night and Day
Eclipse of the Moon	Eclipse Tag
Force of Gravity	Catch the Cane
	Spoon Ball Carry
	Jump the Shot
	Basketball Twenty-One
	Planet Pull (Tide Pull)
Earth's Atmosphere	Hurricane
	Balloon Throw
	Pop the Balloon Relay
	Air Lift
	Water Cycle Relay
Earth's Surface	Zig-Zag Run

Concept: Planet's Orbits Around the Sun

Activity: *Planet Ball* The children form a single circle and count off by two's. The number one's step forward, turn, and face the number two's. The larger circle should be about four feet outside the inner circle. Two children, designated as team captains, stand opposite each other in the circle. The teacher stands in the center of the circle and represents the sun. Each captain has a ball which his team identifies as a planet. On a signal from the teacher, each ball is passed counterclockwise to each team member until it travels all the way around the circle and back to the captain. Any child who is responsible for the ball striking the floor, either through a poor throw or failure to catch the ball, has to recover the ball. As both circles pass the balls simultaneously, the time is kept and recorded. The group that passes the ball around their circle first wins or scores a point. Groups should exchange positions every several rounds.

Application: Prior to playing the game, the children should note that the balls being passed around are the planets and that they are revolving around the sun, represented by the teacher. They should be helped to identify the balls that are being passed counterclockwise because that is the direction the planets orbit the sun. In using this game to illustrate the orbits of planets, it should be stressed that the path or orbit of the ball should be unbroken or uninterrupted. It should also be noted that each completed orbit was done with different amounts of time for each circle, that the inner circle tended to take less time to pass the ball around the circle. Children can be encouraged to find out the difference in the orbits of the planets, as well as the varying lengths of time of these orbits.

Concept: Earth's Orbit Around the Sun

Activity: *Earth's Orbit Relay* The children are arranged in two circles, each circle facing in. A captain is elected for each team, and they stand ready with balls in their hands. On a signal each captain starts his team's ball around by passing to the child on his right. Upon receiving the ball, each child spins around and passes the ball on to the next child on the right. As the ball makes a complete circuit back to the captain, he calls "One." The second time around he calls "Two." This procedure is repeated until the first team to pass the ball around the circle five times wins.

Application: In this game the children need to be helped to see they are dramatizing the way the earth revolves around the sun. The entire circle becomes the complete orbit of the earth. The ball represents the earth, and as it is passed from one child to another, they can see how the earth revolves around the sun. Also, since each child must spin around with the ball before passing it on, the concept of earth's rotation on its axis may be shown. The children must always turn and pass counterclockwise, since that is the direction of the earth's orbit.

Concept: Length of Shadows According to Position of the Sun

Activity: *Shadow Tag* The children are dispersed over the playing area, with one child designated as *It*. If *It* can step on the shadow of one of the children and call his name as he does, that child becomes *It*. A child may keep from being tagged by getting into the shade of a building or tree or by moving in such a way that *It* finds it difficult to step on his shadow.

Application: In playing this game, the class can experiment by playing the game at different times of the day. The children can be helped to note the length of the shadow changes at different times of the day. They might measure and record these observations and seek to determine the reasons for the varying length of the shadows.

Concept: The Turning of the Earth on Its Axis Causes Day and Night

Activity   *Night and Day.* The children stand in a circle
holding hands. One child in the center of the circle
represents the Earth. As the children hold hands,
they chant,

> Illery, dillery, daxis
> The world turns on its axis.
> Isham, bisham bay,
> It turns from night to day.

While the children are chanting, Earth closes his eyes
and turns slowly with one hand pointing towards
the circle of children. As he rotates slowly with eyes
closed (night), he continues to point with his hand.
At the word *day* he stops and opens his eyes (day).
Earth then runs after the child (to whom he is
pointing at the word *day*) around the outside of the
circle until he catches him. When the child is caught,
he becomes the new Earth. The original Earth joins
the circle, and the game continues. It might be
advisable to use a blindfold that the child can slip
off at the end of the verse.

Application: The child in the center became the rotating Earth.
When his eyes were closed, it became night, and
when his eyes were open, it became day. The
children might be encouraged to think of the child
being pointed to as the sun, since it is day when the
eyes are opened, and the sun causes day.

Concept: Eclipse of the Moon

Activity: *Eclipse Tag* The children are grouped by couples
facing each other. The couples are scattered in any
way about the play area. One child is chosen for the
runner and is called Earth. Another child is the
chaser. On a signal the chaser tries to tag Earth.
Earth is safe from being tagged when he runs and
steps between two children who make up a couple.
When Earth steps between the two children, he calls
out "Eclipse." The chaser must then chase the child
in the couple toward whom Earth turns his back. If
the chaser is able to tag Earth, they exchange places.

Application: This activity enables children to dramatize the concept of an eclipse of the moon so that they can see what occurs. The children should be helped to identify that when Earth steps between two children, the one he faces is the moon and his back is turned to the sun, and that the earth's shadow covers the moon.

Concept: Force of Gravity

Activity: *Catch The Cane* The children are arranged in a circle, facing in. Each child is given a number. One child becomes *It* and stands in the center of the circle. He holds a stick or bat upright and balances it by putting his finger on the top of it. *It* calls one of the numbers assigned to the children in the circle. At the same time, he lets go of the stick. The child whose number is called dashes to get the stick before it falls to the ground. *It* dashes to the place occupied by the child whose number was called. If the child gets the stick in time, he returns to his place in the circle, and *It* holds the stick again. After the children have learned the game, several circles can be formed to provide active participation for more children. The teacher can provide for individual differences of poor performers by making the circle smaller.

Application: The stick in this game represents the object which is being acted upon by the force of gravity. Every time *It* lets go of the stick, the stick begins to fall to the ground. This demonstrates the concept of the force of gravity to children. They may be helped to note that they must move faster than the force of gravity in order to catch the stick before it falls to the ground.

Concept: Force of Gravity

Activity: *Spoon Ball Carry* The children are divided into several teams. The teams stand in rows behind a starting line. A large spoon holding a tennis ball is given to the first member of each team. On a given signal they run with the spoons and balls to a designated point and back. They then hand the spoons and balls to the next team members. The team finishing first wins. If a ball drops from a spoon, it must be scooped up with the spoon and not touched otherwise. Some variety can be created by using balls of different sizes and weights. These varying balls can be used at set intervals during one relay or in separate relay races.

Application: The concept of gravity is an inherent part of this activity. The children's attention should be directed as to why the ball seldom drops from the spoon and why, when it does, it falls down, not up. The use of a variety of sizes and weights of balls may create curiosity on the part of the children. Children can be helped to note that they have more success in carrying a larger and heavier ball than one which is smaller and lighter. This experience can be directed toward further research by the children on questions posed by the group.

Concept: Force of Gravity

Activity: *Jump The Shot* The children form a circle with one child in the center. The center child has a length of rope with a beanbag attached to one end. He holds the rope at the other end and swings the rope around close to the ground. The children in the circle must jump over the rope to keep from being hit. Any child who fails to jump and is hit receives a point against him. The child with the least number of points at the end of the game is the winner.

Application: The game is played in small groups, and each child should have a turn to be in the center and swing the rope. The teacher might ask the children what they felt on the other end of the rope as they swung it around, that is, if they felt a pull. The teacher can ask what would happen if the rope broke or they let go of their end. This can be demonstrated. Further questions can lead to what kept the rope and beanbag from flying off during the game, that an inward pull on the rope kept the beanbag moving in a circular pattern. The teacher might also relate this to the manner in which planets travel in a circular orbit around the sun, and the moon around the earth, because of gravitational force.

Concept: Force of Gravity

Activity: *Basketball Twenty-One* The children form teams. The teams make rows behind the free-throw line. The first child takes a shot and scores two points if he makes it. He then recovers the ball and shoots again from closer to the basket. If he makes this shot, he scores one point. The teams take turns at the basket, shooting the long and short shots. The first team reaching twenty-one points wins.

Application: This game can be used during the study of gravitational force. The teacher can demonstrate that the ball must be aimed higher when shooting farther away from the basket to overcome the force of gravity, which pulls the ball toward the earth as it travels through the air. The children can note that if the ball is thrown directly toward the basket without aiming higher to compensate for gravitational pull, the ball will go under the basket. Children can experiment with different types of throws from different distances from the basket.

Concept: Gravitational Pull — Of Tides, Planets

Activity: *Planet Pull (Tide Pull)* The children are divided into two teams. One can be named Earth and the other Moon. The first child on each team kneels down on all fours, facing a member of the other team. There is a line drawn on the floor between them. Each child has a collar made from a towel or piece of strong cloth placed around his neck. Each child grabs both ends of the other person's towel. The object is for each one to try to pull the other one across the line. The child who succeeds scores a point for his team. Each child on the team does the same. The team with the most points wins.

Application: This game can be used to demonstrate the gravitational pull of earth and the moon, or the planets and the sun. It might be pointed out that a large child often was stronger and was usually able to pull a smaller child across the line, just as with members of the solar system being pulled to the largest member, the sun.

Concept: Earth's Atmosphere — Wind Is Moving Air

Activity: *Hurricane* The children are divided into two teams. Each team lines up on either side of a small playing area with lines drawn six feet apart on each side. In the center is a small, light object such as a ping-pong ball. Each child has a fan made of newspaper, cardboard, or some other type of suitable material. On a given signal the children fan the ball toward the opposite goal line. Each time the ball goes over the goal, a point is scored. The team having five points wins the game.

Application: In this activity children can see that their fans create a wind. The wind is moving and makes the ball move. Children might experiment with different types of fans and ways of fanning to see if they can create stronger air movements.

Concept: Earth's Atmosphere — Air Has Pressure and Pushes Against Things

Activity: *Balloon Throw* Children take turns throwing an inflated toy balloon. A line is marked on the floor, and the thrower may use any method of throwing as long as he does not step on or over this line. His throw is measured from the line to the spot his balloon first touches the floor. The child with the longest throw wins.

Application: The children can experience the feeling of throwing an object so light in relation to size that the resistance of air prevents the object from traveling in an arc as expected. In substituting a playground ball, the children can note the difference in the distance it travels with the same type of throw. A tennis ball can also be used for comparison of distance traveled and action of throwing.

Concept: Earth's Atmosphere — Air Takes Up Space and Pushes Against Things

Activity: *Pop The Balloon Relay* The children are divided into relay teams of equal numbers. On the floor beside each child is placed a small balloon that has not been blown up. On a signal the first child on each team runs to the front of the room with his balloon, blows it up and pops it, then returns to his place. When his balloon pops, the next child picks up his, waits for the first child to return to his place, and then. continues in the same manner. The first team to finish with all the team members popping their balloons and returning to their places wins. Since this may be a noisy type relay, it might be advisable to have it outside rather than in the classroom.

Application: As each child blows air into the balloon, he is able to see that the sides of the balloon are pushed out by the air that has filled up the space inside. Likewise, as he pops the balloon, he can see that the air is released and the sides of the balloon are no longer pushed out.

Concept: Earth's Atmosphere — Force or Lift of Air

Activity: *Air Lift* The children are divided into teams of four to six members each. One team stands on one side of a net stretched across the center of the court. (The size of the court may vary.) The game is started by one child throwing a rubber ring over the net. Any opposing team member may catch the ring and throw it back. The ring may not be relayed to another child on the same team. Play continues until a point is scored. A point is scored each time the ring hits the ground in the opponents' court or when any of the following fouls are committed:

1. Hitting the net with the ring.
2. Throwing the ring under the net.
3. Relaying the ring or having two teammates touch

it in succession.

4. Throwing the ring out of bounds if opposing team does not touch it.

The team scored upon puts the ring in play again. Five to fifteen points is a game, depending on the skill of the group.

Application: The ring is used to represent an airplane, and the children's attempts to toss it over the net without allowing it to fall can be compared to *lift.* In attempting to toss the ring over the net, many fouls may be committed, and it should be pointed out that this is due to both the insufficient amount of force of air, the downward pull of gravity, and also poor aiming. In most cases more force or lift is needed to launch a ring, or plane. When each point is made, it can be referred to as a plane successfully launched. The children might be encouraged to find out how planes are launched from aircraft carriers. They may conclude that a plane must have an enormous lift before it can rise. It can be further pointed out that the force that produces the lift to cause a plane to rise is caused by movements of air and that this movement produces low pressures over the top of the wings and high pressures under the bottom of the wings.

Concept: Earth's Atmosphere — Water Cycle

Activity: *Water Cycle Relay* The children are divided into teams of six children each. Each child is assigned a part of the water cycle in the order of the process, for example, (a) water vapor, (b) rain, (c) land, (d) stream, (e) river, and (f) ocean. The teams are seated in rows close enough to be able to pass a ball from one child to the next. On a signal the first child of each team calls his part of the water cycle (water vapor), passes the ball to the second child on his team, and runs to the end of his team's line. The second child calls out his part (rain), passes the ball to the next team member, and moves back in the same manner. This procedure continues until each team has made three complete cycles. The first team to finish wins.

Application: The cycle is represented by the children moving in turn. As the children pass the ball, it should be emphasized that the various stages are represented by each child. It is important that the children note the correct order within the cycle and situate themselves in the line accordingly. The ball represents water regardless of the form it takes within the cycle. The game may be adapted by changing the rain part of the cycle to snow or sleet and by adding brooks and bays if the children so choose.

Concept: Earth's Surface — Coastlines and Mountains Cause Ocean Currents and Winds to Change Direction

Activity: *Zig-Zag Run* The class is divided into teams. The teams form rows behind a starting line. Four ten pins or other objects are placed in a line four feet apart in front of each team. On a signal the first child on each team runs to the right of the first pin and to the left of the second pin and so on in a zig-zag manner. The second child proceeds as the first child. If a child knocks down a pin, he must set it up before he continues. The team finishing first wins.

Application: The children on the teams can represent the ocean currents and winds. The pins can represent the coastlines and mountains. It might be helpful to use children for the objects, and they could change their position slightly each time. The children must go around the objects in order to reach their goal. If the objects were not there, the children could travel in a straight line to the goal and back. By having to go around the objects, children show how the ocean currents and winds have to change direction when they meet obstacles.

CHAPTER EIGHT

LEARNING ABOUT CONDITIONS OF LIFE THROUGH MOTOR ACTIVITY

....

THE following is a summary of the motor activities in this chapter that contain science concepts in the broad area of *Conditions of Life.* Descriptions of the activities as well as an application of each follows the summary.

Concept	*Activity*
Variety of Life	Squirrels in Trees
	Squirrels in Trees (Variation)
	Animal Relay
	Kangaroo Relay
	Snail
	Flowers and Wind
Interdependence of Life	Fox and Geese
	Spider and Flies
	Herds and Flocks
	Fox and Sheep
	Forest Lookout

Concept: Variety of Life — Animals Live in Many Kinds of Homes

Activity: *Squirrels in Trees* With the exception of one child, the children are arranged in groups of three around the activity area. Two of the children in each group face each other and hold hands, forming a hollow tree. The third child is a squirrel and stands between the other two children. The extra child, who is also a squirrel, stands near the center of the activity area. If there is another extra child, there can be two squirrels. The teacher calls, "Squirrel in the tree, listen to me; find yourself another tree." On the last word *tree*, all squirrels must run and get into a different hollow tree, and the extra squirrel also tries to find a tree. There is always one extra squirrel who does not have a tree. At different points in the game, the teacher should have the children change places. The game can be adapted for other animals such as beavers in dams, foxes or rabbits in holes, bears in caves, and the like.

Application: In playing this game, children can name other animals and the kinds of homes in which they live. They can be encouraged to figure out how they could dramatize the different types of homes animals have, e.g. two children forming the hollow tree.

Concept: Variety of Life — Some Animals Hibernate in Winter

Activity: *Squirrels In Trees (Variation)* The regular game of Squirrels in Trees is played. One child is the extra squirrel. The other children stand in groups of three about the play area. In the groups, two of the children face each other and hold hands while the third child, the Squirrel, stands between them. The leader calls out "Squirrel in the tree, listen to me. It is sunny and warm; find yourself something to eat." On the word *eat*, all the squirrels must leave their tree and hunt for food. When the leader calls "Hibernate," all the squirrels, including the extra squirrel, must try to find a hollow tree. There will always be one extra squirrel. The children should be encouraged to be brave while looking for food and not stay too close to a hollow tree.

Application: This variation of the game emphasizes the hibernation concept. By the children dramatizing the concept of food gathering and hibernation, they are helped to see the winter life patterns of some animals.

Concept: Variety of Life — Animals Move About in Different Ways

Activity: *Animal Relay* The children divide into several teams. The teams stand in rows behind a line about twenty feet from a goal line. The object of the relay is for each team member to move forward to the goal line and return to his place at the rear of his team, moving as quickly as he can according to the type of animal movement assigned. Relays may be varied by the children going to the goal line and back doing the following imitations of various animals:

Donkey Walk — traveling on all fours, imitating a donkey's kick and bray.

Crab Walk — walking on all fours, face up.

Bear Walk — walking on all fours, feet going outside of hands.

Rabbit Hop — child moves forward, bringing his feet forward between his hands.

Elephant Walk — child bends forward, hands flat on floor with knees straight and then backwards keeping knees and elbows straight all the time.

On a signal the teams proceed with the relay, using the movement indicated by the teacher. The first team finished wins.

Application: By dramatizing the various movements of animals, children are helped to learn about the differences among animals. Children can be encouraged to figure out ways of moving to represent many types of animals.

Concept: Variety of Life — Animals Move About in Different Ways

Activity: *Kangaroo Relay* The children are divided into several teams. The teams line up in rows behind a starting line. About thirty feet away or less, parallel to the starting line, is a goal line. The first child of each team places the ball between his knees and without touching the ball, jumps to the goal line. He then takes the ball in his hands, runs back to the starting line, and gives the ball to the next child, who must be behind the starting line. The team members proceed in the same manner. The first team finished wins.

Application: Despite their awkard size, kangaroos have an effective means of moving over the ground to escape their enemies. By executing the kangaroo stunt in this game, the children are better able to understand the method of mobility of this animal. The teacher might have the children contrast this method with the way other animals move by acting out different animal movements.

Concept: Variety of Life — Animals Escape Their Enemies in Many Ways

Activity: *Snail* The children stand in a row with the teacher as the leader at the front of the row. While singing the first verse, the teacher walks around in a circle leading the group and continues to walk so that the circle becomes smaller. During the singing of the second verse the leader reverses his direction to enlarge the circle.

> Hand in hand we circle now,
> Like a snail into his shell
> Coming nearer, coming nearer,
> In we go and in we go.
> Aren't you glad this little shell
> Keeps us all and holds us well?

> Hand in hand we circle now,
> Like a snail just from its shell
> Going further, going further,
> Out we go and out we go.
> Aren't you glad this little shell
> Kept us all and held us well?

Application: The concept of animals needing protection from their enemies and employing various means for protection is inherent in this activity. Children might be encouraged to find out other ways animals seek protection from their natural enemies.

Concept: Variety of Life — Wind is Moving Air and Transports Some Kinds of Seeds

Activity: *Flowers And Wind* The children are divided into two teams, each team having a home marked off at opposite ends of a play area with a neutral space between. One team represents a flower (deciding among themselves which flower they shall represent, as daisies, lilies, and so on). They then walk over near the home line of the opposite team. The opposing team (representing the wind) stands in a line within their home area, ready to run. They guess what the flower chosen by their opponents may be. As soon as the right flower is named, the entire team must turn and run home, the wind chasing them. Any children caught by the wind before reaching home must join the wind team. The remaining flowers repeat their play, taking a different flower name each time. This continues until all of the flowers have been caught. The teams then exchange, and the flower team becomes the wind team.

Application: In this game some of the children represent the wind, and the others represent the flowers and/or seeds. As the flowers walk to the wind home, they represent the flower growing through the summer. When the wind guesses the name of the flower, this represents the end of the growth period. As the flowers begin to run, they represent the seeds, and the children chasing them represent the wind carrying the seeds along. The flowers running also represent the seeds dispersing in different directions being borne by the wind.

Concept: Interdependence of Life

Activity: *Fox and Geese* Two lines are drawn on opposite ends of the play area. One child is the fox and stands in the center of the play area. The other children are the geese and stand behind one of the end lines. When the geese are ready, the fox calls

"Run!" and the geese must then run and attempt to cross the opposite end line before the fox can catch them. The geese are not safe until they have crossed this line. The children who are tagged by the fox must help the fox tag the remaining geese the next time. The geese who have not been tagged line up at the end line and, on a signal from the fox, run back to the original starting line. When the geese have run three times, a new fox is chosen.

Application: Through this game the children learn that animals eat other animals as a means of survival and that these types of animals are called carnivorous. The children might find out various animals that are natural enemies and substitute their names for fox and geese.

Concept: Interdependence of Life

Activity: *Spider And Flies* Two goal lines are drawn at opposite ends of the play area and a circle equal distance between the two goal lines. The children stand around the edge of the circle, facing the center. One child, the spider, sits in the center of the circle. The other children are flies. The spider sits very still while the other children (the flies) walk or skip around the circle, clapping their hands as they go. At any time the spider may suddenly jump up and chase the flies. When he does, the flies run toward either goal. A fly tagged before reaching one of the goal lines becomes a spider and joins the first spider in the circle. The original spider always gives the starting signal to chase the flies, and other spiders may not leave the circle to chase the flies until he gives this signal. The last child caught becomes the next spider.

Application: The children should be encouraged to cultivate their quickness. The spider should be urged to leap up suddenly in order to surprise the flies. In this game the children can be helped to understand the interdependence of animals for food by the dramatizing of animals hunting each other for food and the victims seeking shelter for protection.

Concept: Interdependence of Life — Some Animals Live in Social Groups in Which They Work Together to Survive

Activity: *Herds And Flocks* A starting line is drawn. The children are divided into several teams and stand one behind the other in relay formation at the starting line. A goal line is drawn thirty to forty feet in front of the starting line. Each member of the relay team is to perform a different action while going to and from the goal line. The teacher assigns the movement to each team member; for example, the first child on each team is to perform one task, the second child on each team to perform another. Some of the suggested actions are the following:

Walk with stiff knees.

Place hands on hips, hold feet together, and jump.

Proceed in squat position to goal, run to starting line.

Hop on one foot.

Skip to goal, sit on floor, and skip to starting line.

Swing arms in circular motion while walking quickly.

Place hands on head and run.

The signal is given for the first child from each team to proceed with his assigned action. As soon as he returns to the starting line, he touches the extended right hand of the second child on his team and then goes to the end of the line. The second child goes forth performing his designated action. Play continues until one team has had all of its members complete their performances and return to their places. This team is the winner.

Application: The children can learn in playing this game that to win, all the children must cooperate and perform their different actions in an acceptable manner and as quickly as they can. This can be compared with

certain animal groups whose different members
perform various tasks for the safety and well-being
of the group. The concept can be further integrated
into the game by helping children to note that just
as some of the actions in the game are difficult to
do, so are some of the things that have to be done in
order to survive. The children might be encouraged
to find out the various roles different members of
animal groups perform in order to protect the
members of the group from their enemies and to
obtain food. They can be helped to identify which
type of group member is assigned the different roles,
for example, the strong to hunt for food and the
older for lookouts.

Concept: Interdependence of Life — Animals Have To Protect
Themselves From One Another

Activity: *Fox and Sheep* One child is selected to be the fox
who stands in his den, a place marked off on one
side of a play area. The rest of the children are the
sheep. They stand in the sheepfold, another area
marked on the opposite side of the play area. The
remaining part of the play area is called the
meadow. The fox leaves his den and wanders around
the meadow, whereupon the sheep sally forth and
approaching the fox, ask him, "Are you hungry, Mr.
Fox?" Should the fox say "No I am not," the sheep
are safe. When the fox says "Yes I am!" the sheep
must run for the sheepfold, as the fox may then
begin to chase them. The fox tags as many sheep as
he can before they find shelter in the fold. Those
sheep who are caught must go to the fox's den and
thereafter assist the fox in capturing sheep. The
original fox is always the first one to leave the den.
He also is the fox who answers the sheep's questions. The last sheep caught becomes the fox for the
next game. This game can be adapted by using other
animals who are natural enemies to each other as cat
and mouse, hound and rabbit, or fox and geese.

Concept: Interdependence of Life — Conservation of Forests

Activity: *Forest Lookout* The children form a circle and count off by two's. All the one's form a circle; all the two's form a second circle so that there is a double circle with all the children facing inward. The children on the inside circle represent trees. Each member of the outside circle represents a fire fighter and stands behind one of the trees. One child is the Lookout; he stands in the center of the group. The lookout calls loudly, "Fire in the forest! Run, run, run!" while clapping his hands. All the fire fighters in the outside circle begin running to the left. While the fire fighters are running, the lookout quietly takes a place in front of one of the trees. The runners who observe the lookout doing this, do likewise. The fire fighter left without a tree becomes the lookout for the next game, and the trees become the fire fighters for the next game.

Application: This game helps to emphasize the importance of protecting the forests from fire. It can be brought out that many animals lose their homes if the trees burn and that small plants are also destroyed.

LEARNING ABOUT CHEMICAL AND PHYSICAL CHANGES THROUGH MOTOR ACTIVITY

••

T HE following is a summary of the motor activities in this chapter that contain science concepts in the broad area of *Chemical and Physical Changes.* Descriptions of the activities as well as an application of each follows the summary.

Concept	*Activity*
Chemical and Physical Changes	Water-Water
	Molecule Ball
	Molecule Pass
	Boiling Water
	Tag and Stoop
	Oxygen and Fuel
Light	Light Bounce
	Heat and Light
	Spectrum Relay
Energy	
Machines	Wheelbarrow
	Tug of War
	Pin Guard
	Balloon Ball
	Siamese Twins
	Shoe Box Relay
	Hot Potato

	Net Ball
Electricity	Straddle Ball Roll
	Electric Ball
	Current Relay
	Lightning Relay
	Keep Away
Magnetism	Link Tag
	Hook-On Tag
	North and South
	Magnet, Magnet

CHEMICAL AND PHYSICAL CHANGES

Concept: Molecular Structure of Water (H_2O)

Activity: *Water-Water* The children form a circle holding hands and one member is *It* and stands in the center of the circle. (*It* represents oxygen.) *It* tries to break out of the circle between children by trying to make them break their grip. If *It* succeeds in breaking through the circle, he immediately runs in either direction around the circle pursued by both of the members who broke the chain. If *It* is tagged by either of the other two members before he can return to one of their places in the circle, he has to try to break out of the circle again or another child can be selected to be *It*. If *It* eludes the chasers and returns to the circle before being tagged, the last chaser turns to the circle and can become *It*.

Application: The simple structure of water can be used as an introduction to molecular structure of matter. Discussion can relate this game to the structure of water, that is hydrogen (two parts) oxygen (one part). With the circle representing a molecule of water and *It* representing one part of oxygen, and the two chasers representing two parts of hydrogen, the children can get a feel for a better understanding of molecular structure of other elements of matter.

Concept: Movement of Molecules in Solids, Liquids, and Gases

Activity: *Molecule Ball* The children arrange themselves in a circle. The group then counts off by two's. The number one's face inward, and the number two's face outward, i.e. one's and two's are facing each other. Each captain has a ball that is to be moved around the circle until it travels back to the captain. The exact manner in which the balls are to be moved around the circles is determined by the leader calling "solid," "liquid," or "gas." When "gas" is called, the ball is to be thrown from one child to the next; when "liquid" is called, the ball is to be bounced from one child to the next; and when "solid" is called, the ball is to be passed to the next child. When the ball completes the circle, that team which does so first is declared the winner. Whenever a child drops or does not catch the ball passed to him, he must retrieve the ball, return to his place in the circle, and then continue to move the ball to the next child.

Application: The use of *solid, liquid,* and *gas* as call words to change the speed of the balls' progress around the circles emphasizes the difference in speed of molecule's movement in solids, liquids, and gases. The children can be helped to note that the method of moving the ball around the circle relates to the speed of the movement of molecules in these different states of matter.

Concept: Molecules Are in Rapid and Ceaseless Motion

Activity: *Molecule Pass* The class is divided into four groups, with each group standing in a straight line. The four groups form a rectangle with each group representing one side of the rectangle. The captain of each group stands near the center of the rectangle in front of his group. On a signal each captain throws his ball to his group, starting at the right. As each child receives the ball, he throws it back to his captain and assumes a squatting position. When the captain throws the ball to the last child in his group, he runs to the right of his group as the rest of the children stand. The last child on the left runs with the ball to the captain's place, and the procedure is repeated.

Application: Each ball represents a molecule of matter. The balls are kept in motion at all times. The children can be helped to note that the ball (the molecule of matter) has to be kept moving. This can lead to a discussion of molecules of different substances: the greater space and rapid movement of molecules of gases (depending on area temperature), the less space and less rapid movement of molecules of liquids, and the lesser space and least rapid movement of molecules of solids.

Concept: Elements in a Compound (the Composition of Molecules) Cannot Be Separated by Physical Means

Activity: *Boiling Water* Two or more circles are formed. Each circle is given one or more balls. A kitchen cooking pot is set along the sidelines of the play area. One child in each circle is the leader. When the teacher calls "cold water," the children in each circle pass the ball from one child to the next. Whenever the teacher calls "warm water," the children roll the ball across the center of the circle from one to another. If the teacher calls "boiling water," the children throw the ball to different ones in the circle. When the teacher calls "water vapor," the ball is immediately thrown to the circle leader, who then runs with it to the kitchen pot on the sidelines. The team whose leader reaches the pot first wins.

Application: The ball represents a molecule of water. The ball is one of the surface molecules. At first, the molecule moves slowly (cold water). When the water begins to warm up, the speed of the molecule increases (warm water). As the water approaches boiling point, the speed of molecules increases (boiling water) until it acquires sufficient motion to escape to the air (water vapor). The ball (molecule) has not been altered. It has moved from one place (the liquid state or water) to another place (gaseous state or water vapor).

Concept: Chain Reaction Comes from One Molecule Hitting Another (or Neutrons in Radioactive Materials)

Activity: *Tag and Stoop* The children are scattered over the playing area. One child is *It* and tries to tag two children, one with each hand. When *It* tags the first child, he then grasps the hand of that child. The two continue running after other children until *It* is able to tag a second child. *It* then stands still and gets down in a stooping position. The two children tagged now each try to tag two others and then they stoop down. The four children tagged now continue in the same manner. The object of the game is to see how long it takes for everyone to be tagged.

Application: In trying to demonstrate chain reaction, the increasingly powerful effect of a small beginning should be brought out. As the children watch the spread of those who are being tagged, they can see this effect.

Concept: Burning Is Oxidation: The Chemical Union of a Fuel with Oxygen

Activity: *Oxygen And Fuel* One child is chosen to be fuel and another child is oxygen. The remaining children join hands and form a circle, with fuel in the center of the circle and oxygen on the outside of the circle. The children in the circle try to keep oxygen from getting into the circle and catching fuel. If oxygen gets in the circle, the children in the circle then let fuel out of the circle and try to keep oxygen in, but they must keep their hands joined at all times. When oxygen catches fuel, the game is over, and they join the circle while two other children become fuel and oxygen. If fuel is not caught in a specified period of time, a new oxygen can be selected.

Application: One child represents the fuel (as trees in a forest) and another the oxygen (the air). The children in the circle are the preventers of fire. If oxygen catches fuel and ignites him by tagging him, a fire is started. Then the game is over. In this manner children can be helped to note that oxygen feeds fires and that oxygen must be kept from fires that have been started in order to put them out. The children might be encouraged to find out ways that fires are smothered, depending upon the type of burning material.

LIGHT

Concept: When Light Strikes a Solid Object, It Bounces.

Activity: *Light Bounce* The children are divided into several teams. Two lines are marked on the floor or play area, parallel to a blank wall. One line is drawn six inches from the wall and is the goal line. The second line is drawn twelve feet from the wall. Behind this second line, the teams stand in rows. Each team is given a small wooden block. The first child on each team takes turns throwing his block. If the block lands between the goal line and the wall, a point is scored for that team. If the block falls outside the goal line, each other team gets one point. Each child on the teams proceeds in the same manner until each child has had a throw. The team with the highest score wins.

Application: Children can be helped to note that the wooden blocks rebound from the wall just as light rays do upon coming in contact with a solid object.

Concept: Heat and Light Can Be Reflected

Activity: *Heat and Light* The children are divided into several teams. The teams make rows at a specified distance from the blank wall of a building. The first child on each team throws a ball against the building and catches it as it bounces back to him, passes it over his head to the next child on the team, and then moves to the end of the line. The team to complete the procedure first wins.

Application: Attention can be called to the fact that just as the ball hits the wall and bounces back, so light and heat are reflected, e.g. light and heat are reflected (or bounced off) by a mirror or other shiny surface.

Concept: A Prism Can Separate a Beam of White Light Into a Spectrum

Activity: *Spectrum Relay* The class is divided into two teams so that there will be seven children on each team. Each team forms a row behind a starting line. Then the children on each team are assigned a specific color of the spectrum and stand in the correct order that colors appear in the spectrum, e.g. red, orange, yellow, green, blue, indigo, and violet. Each child is given the appropriate color tag to pin on his clothing so that his teammates can quickly see where to line up. Those children who are not assigned to a relay team are the prism and stand at a given distance away from the starting line and space themselves several feet apart, facing the relay teams. On a signal all the children on each team must run between and around back of the children standing a distance away (the prism) and return to the starting line. The team members must then join hands so that each team finishes by being lined up in the correct order of colors in the spectrum behind the starting line. The first team lined up correctly behind the starting line wins. A few children may change places with those who did not have a chance to run in the first relay.

Application: This relay provides children with the opportunity to dramatize the concept of the prism. The teams represent the beams of light before passing through the glass prism (represented by the children standing a distance away) and that after they passed through the glass prism, they then represented the band of colors called the visible spectrum. During the discussion it can be pointed out that each color of light travels through the glass prism at a different speed. The children can be encouraged to find about different things in nature that serve as prisms to create visible spectrums.

ENERGY

Concept: Heavy Load Can Be Moved More Easily By Use of Machines

Activity: *Wheelbarrow* This is a couple stunt and each child has a partner of about equal size and strength. One child assumes a position with his hands on the floor, with his arms straight and his feet extended behind him. The other child picks up the feet of the first child who keeps his knees straight. The first child becomes a wheelbarrow by walking along on his hands while the other child holds on to his legs. The children change positions so that each can become a wheelbarrow. Couples can perform separately or teams can be formed to run a wheelbarrow relay.

Application: This activity can help the children understand how machines can make work easier. The child acting as the wheelbarrow will see that he is doing more work while the child operating the wheelbarrow uses very little effort.

Concept: Energy Is Needed To Stop Rapidly Moving Objects (Newton's Law of Inertia)

Activity: *Jump The Brook Relay* The children are divided into teams. The teams stand in rows behind the starting line. The goal line is a good running distance away. Two lines, approximately three feet apart, are drawn parallel about ten feet from the goal line. The space between the two center lines represents the brook. On a signal the captain of each team runs to the brook, stops, jumps over the brook with two feet together, runs to the finish line, and then returns to the starting line in the same way. He touches the second child on his team and then goes to the rear of his team. This procedure is continued until all the team members have jumped the brook. The team finishing first wins. Any child who fails to jump the brook (and so falls in) must return to the starting line and begin his turn again. The teacher may therefore adjust the size of the brook according to the limitations of the group.

Application: Children can discover that it takes great effort on their part to stop themselves when they reach the brook in order to make their jump with two feet together. When they stop suddenly, they find that while they might be able to stop their feet, the upper part of their bodies continues to move forward. Actually trying to stop on their part involves body energy or force. The children can also be encouraged to experiment and find that the faster they run, the more energy they have to expend to stop themselves.

Concept: Principle of Inertia

Activity: *Tug Of War* The class is divided into two teams. A line is drawn between the teams as a goal line. The teams line up on each side of the goal line. Each member grabs hold of the rope in a single file fashion at the same distance from the goal line. Both teams are now in position to pull against each other. On a signal they begin pulling. The team that pulls the other over the goal the first wins the game.

Application: If each team in the Tug of War pulls just as hard as the other, there is no motion in either direction. If one team is stronger than the other, then there will be an unbalanced force, causing the other team to be pulled over the goal line in the direction of the stronger team.

Concept: A Body Left to Itself, Free from the Action of Other Bodies, Will, if at Rest, Remain at Rest

Activity: *Pin Guard* The children form a circle. Ten pins or other suitable objects are set up in the middle of the circle. One child is selected as a guard to protect the pins. On a signal the children start rolling a ball to knock over the pins. The guard tries to keep the ball away from the pins by kicking it back toward the circle. The child who succeeds in knocking down a pin becomes the new guard.

Application: The pins in this game represent the body at rest (inertia) and the ball the force that puts the body in motion. It can be pointed out to the children that the pins in the center of the circle remain at rest until an outside force (the ball) strikes the pins and puts them in motion.

Concept: Laws of Motion (Acceleration Is in Proportion to the Force That Caused It and in the Same Direction as That Force)

Activity: *Balloon Ball* The class is divided into two teams. Each team divides into three groups. If a classroom is used, rows one, three, and five are team A. Rows two, four, and six are team B. The space on the outside of the first and sixth row are the goals. If the game is played outside, the teams may sit in the same manner with lines drawn outside the first and sixth row to serve as goal lines. A balloon is tossed into the air in the center of the room by the teacher. The seated children strike the balloon with the open hand and try to get it over their opponent's goal. The children may not strike the balloon with their fists or leave their seats. If either of these violations is committed, the balloon is tossed into the air by a member of the team that committed the violation. Each goal counts one point. The team scoring the greater number of points wins the game. If too many goals are made, one child from each team may be chosen to be goalkeeper. They may stand and try to prevent the balloon from striking the floor in their respective goal areas.

Application: It can be pointed out to the children that when they hit the balloon, the balloon moves in the same direction as their hand. They also can be helped to notice that if the balloon is tapped lightly, it moves a short distance, and if it is hit hard, the balloon moves a long distance. This game dramatizes the concepts involved in Newton's laws of motion in a way children can see and understand.

Concept: Friction

Activity: *Siamese Twins* The children get in pairs and sit back to back with arms folded and legs extended straight ahead and together. The object is to see which pair can stand first with feet together while maintaining the folded arm position.

Application: Before the game children can talk about some of the results of friction, such as heat and the resulting problems confronting scientists who design space missiles. The class might discuss ways in which friction helps us, i.e. the friction between feet and ground when we walk and how we use snow tires or chains to provide friction in snow and icy weather. During and after this game the teacher can help the children see how the friction of their feet against the floor keeps them from sliding down. After the game the children might plan to chart lists of ways in which friction helps us.

Concept: Friction

Activity: *Shoe Box Relay* The class is divided into several teams. The teams stand in rows behind a starting line twenty to thirty feet away from a goal line. Each team is given two large shoe boxes. The first child places his feet in the shoe boxes and advances to the goal line by sliding his feet along in a walking motion. When he crosses the goal line, he then returns to the starting line. The second child then places his feet in the shoe boxes and proceeds in the same manner. The first team to complete the race with all the team members in line behind the starting line wins. It is a good idea to have extra shoe boxes in case one becomes mutilated.

Application: From this activity the chidren can be shown that friction occurs whenever two surfaces rub together, and the larger the two areas moving against each other, the greater the friction. The children might discuss how tired their legs get and how much more difficult this means of locomotion is than walking.

Concept: Machines Make Work Easier—Arm as Lever

Activity: *Hot Potato* The class is divided into even number lines of five to six children each, separated at arms length from each other. Each line faces another line five to twenty feet away. Each child has a turn holding a ball at chest height in one hand and hitting it with the palm of the other hand, directing the ball to the line facing him. Each child of the opposite line scores one point for each ball he catches. The child who catches the ball then proceeds to hit the ball back to the opposite line, and a child tries to catch the ball to score a point. The child with the highest score wins.

Application: The use of the arm as a lever can be demonstrated in this activity. The teacher might draw a picture on the blackboard to show children how the arm works as a lever.

Concept: The Lever (In the Third-Class Lever the Effort Is Placed Between the Load and the Fulcrum)

Concept: The Greater a Force Applied to a Mass, the Greater the Acceleration of That Mass Will Be

Activity: *Net Ball* (Note: Two concepts can be developed by Net Ball.) Before the activity the children can be told that serving is a basic skill used in the game of net ball and that for a successful game of net ball, it is necessary to learn to serve the ball properly. The server stands on the end line facing the net. He holds the ball in his left hand about waist height in front of him and to the right. He hits the ball underhand with his right hand (heel of the hand or fist). The weight of his body is transferred forward to the left foot as the right arm moves forward in a follow-through movement.

The children are divided into two groups, each group spaced in a pattern on one side of the net facing the other group. After the teacher demonstrates several times, each child is given the opportunity to attempt to serve the ball two or three times. Following practice, the game is started by one child serving the ball over the net. Any opposing team member may hit the ball with his hands (heel of the hand or fist) back to the other side of the net. The ball may not be relayed to another child on the same team. Play continues until a point is scored. A point is scored each time the ball hits the ground in the opponents' court or any of the following fouls are committed:

1. Hitting the net with the ball.
2. Hitting the ball under the net.
3. Relaying the ball or having two teammates touch it in succession.
4. Hitting the ball out of bounds if opposing team does not touch it.

Application: (The Lever) During the practice it can be shown how the arm has acted as a lever in the serving action, that the elbow joint was the fulcrum, the forearm was the effort, and the ball was the load. Children can then be encouraged to find other examples that would illustrate this type of lever, i.e. a man swinging a golf club or a boy swinging at a ball with a bat.

Application: (Force and Acceleration) It can be noted that the servers have difficulty getting the ball in the opposite court, that the ball either fails to go over the net or it is hit out of bounds on the opposite side. The teacher can stop the activity to ask what makes the ball go out of bounds. The children might note that it was hit too hard. If the ball fails to go over the net, it can be pointed out it was not hit hard enough. The teacher can then ask the class to explain what factor influences the speed and distance the ball travels (the force of the serve or how hard the ball is hit that governs the acceleration of the ball). The children can be encouraged to apply this concept to other types of activities such as batting a baseball, peddling a bike, or a rocket booster.

Concept: Electrical Current Must Travel in a Circuit

Activity: *Straddle Ball Roll* The children line up one behind the other in teams of eight to ten. All stand with their feet apart. The leader of each team holds a basketball or a similar-sized rubber playground ball. On a signal the leader stoops and rolls the ball back between the legs of all the members of his team. When the last player on the team secures the ball, he holds it up. The team getting the ball up first wins one point. The last child of each team now moves up to be the leader. On a signal he rolls the ball and again the last child on the team holds it up as soon as he gets it. A scorer at the blackboard or out-of-doors keeps track of the points made for each team. The team making the most points after all have had a turn to roll the ball wins the game.

Application: The ball is the current of electricity. The first member of each team is the source, and the circuit is the path between the children's feet and legs. The first child might be considered the switch to turn on the current. The circuit may be broken if the ball goes outside a child's legs. (A point might be scored against the team if this occurs.) The electrical current continues (the ball being put back into play) when the circuit is repaired.

Concept: Electricity Is the Flow of Electrons in a Closed Circuit

Activity: *Electric Ball* The children form a circle and join hands (representing a closed circuit). The children are to move a soccer ball or similar type ball if a soccer ball is not available around the inside of the circle. The ball represents the current or flow of electrons. The children move the ball from one child to the next by using the instep of the foot as in soccer. The object of the game is to keep the ball moving around the circle and preventing the ball from leaving the circle by blocking it with the feet or legs while keeping the hands joined at all times. If the ball leaves the circle (an open or broken circuit), the two children between whom the ball escapes the circle are each given a point. The game continues with the children having the lowest scores as winners.

Application: Children are able to see this concept demonstrated in this game, that of the flow of electrons through a closed circuit by passing the ball around the circle and that a broken circuit prevents the flow of electricity when the ball leaves the circle.

Concept: Electricity Is the Flow of Electrons in a Closed Circuit

Activity: *Current Relay* Children are arranged in teams in rows. Each child reaches back between his legs with his right hand and grasps the left hand of the child immediately in back of him. On a signal the teams thus joined together race to the goal line some thirty to forty feet from the starting line and then race back to the starting line. The team finishing first with the line unbroken wins.

Application: The joined hands of the members of the teams represent the closed circuit. As long as the circuit remains unbroken, electricity can flow (the children could move their feet and proceed with the race). If the circuit is broken, it has to be repaired (the children rejoin hands) before electricity can continue to flow and the team can move forward again.

Concept: Lightning Is Electricity

Activity: *Lightning Relay* The class is divided into several teams. The first child in each team toes a starting line. On a signal he jumps. Someone marks the heel print of each jumper. The next child on each team steps forward to the heel mark of the first child, toes this mark, and jumps. This procedure is continued until every child on each team has jumped. The team having jumped the greatest distance wins.

Application: Each child is electricity of lightning jumping from one cloud to another. The concept of lightning being electricty gathering in a cloud and jumping to the ground or to another cloud can be noted by the children as they dramatize it in the game.

Concept: Electricity Flows Along Metal Conductors and Will Not Flow Along Nonmetal Conductors Such as Glass or Rubber

Activity: *Keep Away* If there is a large number of children, they should form a circle. For a small group the children may spread out and form a square or five-sided figure. One child is chosen to be *It,* and he stands in the center. The other children throw a ball around the circle or across the square. They try to keep the ball away from *It* while he tries to get his hands on it. If *It* catches the ball, he changes places with the last child who threw it, and the game continues. If *It* is unable to get hold of the ball in a minute's time, another *It* can be chosen.

Application: The ball becomes the electricity, the ball throwers are the conductors, and *It* is a nonconductor who tries to interfere with the flow of electricity. Any time the nonconductor is successful in interfering, the current of electricity is interrupted. Children can be encouraged to find out the kind of materials that are nonconductors and several safety practices that have developed for those working around electricity, both in business and around the home.

Concept: A Magnet Attracts Iron and Steel

Activity: *Link Tag* The children are scattered about the play area. Two children are chosen to be the taggers. The taggers link hands and attempt to tag other children. All children tagged link hands between the first two taggers, the chain growing longer with each addition. Only the end children, the original taggers, may tag other children. Runners may crawl under the chain to escape being tagged, but any child who deliberately breaks the chain is automatically caught. The game continues until all the children are tagged. The last two children caught become the taggers for the next game.

Application: The taggers are the magnets, and the other children represent things made of iron or steel. As the taggers touch the other children by tagging, the children are attracted to them and become a part of the magnetic chain. It should also be pointed out that only the taggers at the ends of the chain can tag others which demonstrates that magnets are strongest at the ends or poles.

Concept: The Force of a Magnet Will Pass Through Many Materials

Activity: *Hook-on Tag* One child is selected as a runner or magnet. The remaining children form groups of four. The children in each group stand one behind the other, each with arms around the waist of the child in front. The runner attempts to hook on at the end of any column where he can. The group members twist and swing about, trying to protect the end person from being caught. If the runner is successful, the leader of that group becomes the new runner. The group having the most of its original members in it at the end of a specified period of time is the winner.

Application: Before starting the game, it should be pointed out that the runner in the game is the magnet. When he is successful in hooking on to the end of one of the groups, the power of the magnet travels through the group to the first person, who becomes the new magnet. This activity dramatizes that a magnet does not have to be in direct contact with another magnetic material in order to attract it. Later, children can be encouraged to experiment to determine which materials the force of a magnet will travel through.

Concept: Unlike Poles of a Magnet Attract Each Other

Activity: *North and South* The class is divided into two equal groups. The two groups line up facing each other about ten feet apart midway between designated goal lines. One group is named North and the other one South. The teacher has a ten-inch square of cardboard which has N on one side and an S on the other. The teacher throws the cardboard into the air between the teams where all can see it as it lands. If the S side shows, the South team turns and runs to their goal line, chased by the North team. All who are tagged before reaching the line join North, and the two groups line up facing each other again. The cardboard is thrown in the air again, and the game continues in the same manner. The team which eliminates the other wins the game.

Application: The two groups represent the opposite or unlike poles of a magnet, the N and S poles. When one group turns to run to its goal line, it attracts the other group which pursues it.

Concept: When a Magnet Attracts an Object, That Object Becomes a Magnet

Activity: *Magnet, Magnet* The children are divided into groups called pins, needles, paper clips, or anything else that can be attracted by a magnet. The groups stand behind a line at one end of the play area. One child is selected to be the magnet and stands in the center of the play area. The magnet calls, "Magnet, magnet. I dare pins come over" (or any of the other groups), whereupon all the children of that group run to the opposite side of the play area. Magnet tries to catch them. Any child tagged must then help magnet whenever he calls another group to come over. The magnet may dare everybody over at one time or two groups at a time. The last child caught becomes the new magnet.

Application: The children should note that the magnet, as he tags other children, causes them to become magnetized and have the power to magnetize others by tagging them. The magnet attracts others by calling to them.

INDEX

A

Ammons, R. B., 22
Aristotle, 46
Armington, John C., 24
Asher, James J., 14, 15

B

Basal metabolic rate, 20
Beck, Robert H., 7
Bilodeau, Edward A., 23
Bilodeau, Ina, 23
Blackwood, Paul E., 7
Blough, Glenn O., 7
Brown, J. S., 22

C

Comenius, 46
Cook, Walter W., 7
Cramer, Roscoe V., 29
Cruikshank, William M., 87
Current practices in elementary school
    science, 9-10

D

Developing science concepts through
    motor activity in broad units of
    study, 39-45
Dewey, John, 26, 46
Domian, Otto E., 29
Dywab, Gunnar, 84

F

Factors influencing learning through
    motor activity, 18-26
    motivation, 20-24
    proprioception, 24-25
    reinforcement, 25-26

Featherstone, W. B., 84, 89
Froebel, 46

G

Good, Carter V., 11, 20

H

Hall, G. Stanley, 46
Herrick, Virgil E., 30
Hicks, Wm. Vernon, 5, 62
Humphrey, James H., 12, 15, 27, 54, 56,
    58, 65, 67, 81, 90
Hunter, Edward, 27

I

Integration of science and reading, 62
Ison, Charles F., 55
Ivanitchkii, M. F., 27

J

Jacks, L. P., 46
Johnson, C. Orville, 87
Johnson, Doris J., 85
Johnson, G. B., 13
Johnson, W. R., 13

K

Kearney, Nolan C., 7
Keith, Lowell G., 29
Kirk, Samuel A., 84, 88

L

Learning about chemical and physical
    changes through motor activity,
    112-130

131